A GUIDE TO AMERICAN FOLKLORE

A GUIDE *to* AMERICAN FOLKLORE

LEVETTE J. DAVIDSON

Professor of English
University of Denver

GREENWOOD PRESS, PUBLISHERS
NEW YORK

PREFACE

Folklore is of many varieties. People are interested in it for diverse reasons; it serves numerous ends. But all folklorists agree that it is a fascinating subject, and that it adds to their understanding of human nature and to their delight in the daily spectacle of diverse ways of living.

Moreover, an accurate and sympathetic understanding of the traditional cultures of the various peoples of the United States and of the rest of the world is needed more than ever. If understanding and good will are to replace hatred and bitter rivalry as bases for our many relationships, we shall need all of the tools that can be made to serve in bringing about this change. We come close to the nature of a people when we learn their songs and ballads, folktales, proverbs, riddles, customs, and popular beliefs. While the learned tradition contains the common heritage accumulated by various civilizations, the folk tradition cherishes differences which individualize group ways of life. If understood, these differences add the spice of variety but are not allowed to serve as barriers. Instead, comparative studies in folklore provide a bridge from one folk culture to another.

Americans have, during the past decade or two, become more and more conscious that they possess a rich heritage of folklore. Some of the folk songs and ballads, popular tales and legends, picturesque customs and costumes, graceful dances, folk arts and crafts, traditional beliefs, and vivid ways of speech were brought to the shores of North America by emigrants; other folk expressions developed out of the life of the common people in the new environment, in response to basic and universal human interests, but shaped by new backgrounds, new occupations, and new events.

Although many collections of various kinds of American folklore, numerous scholarly studies, some useful bibliographies, and several fine journals of folklore are in existence, no comprehensive guide to American folklore has been available. The present work is designed to meet the needs of general readers and of students who wish to explore the various parts of this field of knowledge. Accordingly, definitions of each type of folklore are given, together with a list of the important books covering each subject, and a number of suggestions for further study and for collecting. With such material as a basis each reader can then follow up his special interests. Knowing what is already available in print and how it is interpreted by scholars, he can better understand the value of the folk elements in his own everyday life, in the lives of various special groups in America, and in the popular cultural heritage from America's past.

One might justify the collecting and the study of folklore today as a harmless type of antiquarian escape from the pressures of modern living. It is, however, wiser to cultivate folklore as one more tool in the attempt to understand and to solve modern problems. Any knowledge or activity that helps us to bridge the chasms between people separated by differences in race, in cultural background, in economic status, and in vocational activity should be utilized to the fullest extent possible. Democracy rests upon an intelligent and sympathetic recognition of the dignity and the worth of all human beings.

The Twentieth Century has been called "The Century of the Common Man." The trend in the United States and in many other parts of the world seems to be in the direction of greater and greater emphasis upon the welfare type of statism, in which control is, theoretically at least, in the hands of the masses of people and the state is evaluated according to its program for promoting the security, the equality of treatment, the prosperity, and the contentment of all. Therefore it becomes imperative that political, educational, and artistic leadership, if it is to be most wise and efficient, should know not only the common man's physical and economic problems but also his emotional, intellectual, aesthetic, and even spiritual needs—what they are, how they have expressed themselves in the past, how they have been modified by physical and social environment, what have been creative and rewarding expressions and developments and what have been destructive and frustrating manifestations and influences.

Evidence in regard to popular culture should be assembled and analyzed, and critical judgment should be applied, in order to produce conclusions that are sound and in order to provide some guidance for present and future action and planning. Experimentation can demonstrate the value or lack of value of such conclusions. But the existence of a body of evidence concerning folk life of relatively recent times cannot fail to reveal much of use as hypothesis and example.

Folklore is also a storehouse from which modern authors, visual artists, and musicians may draw usable materials and inspiration. Folk artists have portrayed the feelings, attitudes, beliefs, sorrows, and aspirations of everyday life in all ages and all cultures, thus adding to our common heritage of human understanding and aesthetic experience. Teachers and social workers continue to use folklore in the promotion of better relationships among diverse cultural groups. But folklore students need no further justification than the intrinsic merit of folk materials as entertainment and as human expression.

American folklore, in the literal sense of the phrase, includes the folklore of native Indian tribes, of the Spanish-speaking peoples of Central and South America, of the French-speaking peoples of Canada, and of numerous other "foreign-language" groups. But the present work concentrates upon the folklore of the English-speaking people of the United States. Numerous references concerning the folklore of the omitted groups are, however, listed in the bibliographies and should be consulted by those ready to engage upon comparative studies or by those who have the linguistic tools needed.

The author remembers with gratitude the stimulus and the cooperation that he has received from the lively members of his classes in "American Folklore" at the University of Denver, from the sympathetic administrators and colleagues at the University, from the richly gifted participants in the annual Western Folklore Conferences, from the devoted American folklore collectors and scholars in various regions of our land, and from the innumerable relatives, friends, acquaintances, and even strangers who as carriers of folklore yielded—often unknowingly—priceless examples of our living traditions and lore.

Valuable aid in preparing the final copy of this guide was furnished by Frank Merchant and Ann Williams, graduate students in the University of Denver at the time. Grateful acknowledgment, also, is made for assistance provided from The Research Fund of the University of Denver.

Levette J. Davidson

Denver, Colorado
September 15, 1950

CONTENTS

CHAPTER ONE

WHAT IS FOLKLORE?

Definitions and Comments

Folklore is the popular heritage of a group held to-gether by common interests. It includes legends, tales, songs, beliefs, homely wisdom, common ways of speaking, jests, games, festivals, music, dances, customs, crafts, folk arts, etc. It is to be distinguished from the learned tradition taught in schools and from commercially developed materials, although these too contain much that originated with the folk. One acquires his folklore—unless he becomes a systematic student or a scientific collector of folk expressions—by hearsay and by imitation, not from the printed page or as a purchasable commodity.

Originally unrecorded except in the memories and the habits of the common people themselves, a vast amount of folklore has now been assembled from all parts of the United States, as it has in Europe and elsewhere. Much of this is available in print, for the information and the pleasure of an increasing body of readers. But not all of the folklore surviving from earlier times has been captured, nor has the development of new folklore ceased. Scholarly activity today includes, therefore, additional collecting, archiving, and publication as well as the study and critical evaluation of earlier examples.

The study of folklore leads one into many fields. Ballads, songs, folk tales, and legends may be considered in relationship to parallel types of standard literature; folk speech, folk sayings, and dialects are subjects for linguistic research; popular customs, beliefs, and bits of folk wisdom may be explained by the aid of psychology and sociology and may even contribute to these sciences; folk arts and crafts may inspire new directions in the fine arts. Anthropology, philosophy, religion, and history are other learned disciplines that cover many of the fields of human activity that the folklorist also approaches; but he has his own special purposes or points of view and his own somewhat different methods.

It is difficult to reach a satisfactory definition of folklore; but in general the term is applied to the traditional expressions of unsophisticated groups of people, expressions that are oral or informal in transmission, that are of unknown or forgotten origin, that are the personal property of no one and that have been subject to modification while being communicated. Folklore thrives best among isolated, homogeneous, and unlearned societies; but aside from survivals, much folklore appears today as the living traditions of special groups in a high state of civilization and sophistication, such as clubs, fraternities, schools, and workers in a common vocation. We all, more or less, follow folk patterns, enjoy folk creations, and pass along folklore.

The term *folklore* was coined in 1846 by the Englishman William John Thoms to replace the phrase "Popular Antiquities, or Popular Literature." Nearly a century earlier, Bishop Thomas Percy had popularized the collecting of English and Scottish ballads; and in 1812-15 Grimm brothers in Germany issued their epoch-making book of children's household tales. In America Professor

2

Francis J. Child, of Harvard, published his scholarly edition of *The English and Scottish Popular Ballads* from 1882 to 1898. American folklore studies were firmly established by the appearance in 1888 of the *Journal of American Folklore* as the official organ of the American Folklore Society. Space does not permit further tracing of the development of folklore activities by American scholars, amateur collectors, popular entertainers, and creative artists; but it is widely recognized today that folklore is a vital part of our American heritage and that it plays a significant role in our regional and national ways of living.

Since folklorists differ in their definitions of folklore, the student should compare the ideas contained in several different references. Actual collections of various types of folklore serve best as illustrations of what is considered to be folklore by active workers. By running through past issues of the folklore journals, listed below, a reader can find many significant discussions of folklore theory as well as articles containing examples of nearly every kind of collectable materials.

Basic Reading* and General References

Beckwith, Martha W., *Folklore in America: Its Scope and Method.** Vassar Folklore Foundation, Poughkeepsie, N. Y., 1931 (Out of print).

Boggs, Ralph S., "Folklore Bibliography." Annual feature of *Southern Folklore Quarterly*, 1938 +.

Benedict, Ruth, "Folklore," in *Encyclopedia of the Social Sciences.** Macmillan, N. Y., 1931.

Botkin, Ben A., *A Treasury of American Folklore.** Crown, N. Y., 1944.

————————, and Lomax, Alan, "Folklore, American," in "Ten Eventful Years," *Encyclopaedia Brittanica*, Chicago, 1947.

Clough, Ben C., *The American Imagination at Work.* Knopf, N. Y., 1947.

Hand, Wayland D., "Folklore," in "American Bibliography," in *Publications of the Modern Language Association of America.* N. Y., 1930-1937.

Herskovits, Melville J., "Folklore after a Hundred Years: A Problem in Redefinition," *Journal of American Folklore*, 59, April-June, 1946.

————————, *Man and His Works: The Science of Cultural Anthropology.** Knopf, N. Y., 1948.

Krappe, Alexander H., *The Science of Folk Lore.** The Dial Press, N. Y., 1930 (out of print).

Leach, Maria, *et. al., Standard Dictionary of Folklore, Mythology, and Legend.** Funk and Wagnalls, N. Y., I, 1949, II, 1950. cf. I, pp. 398-403 for definitions of folklore.

Lomax, Alan and Cowell, Sidney Robertson, *American Folk Song and Folklore.* Progressive Education Association, Service Center Pamphlet, N. Y., 1942.

4

Memoirs of the American Folklore Society. American Folklore Society, University of Pennsylvania, Philadelphia, 1894 +.

*Opportunities in Arizona Folklore.** University of Arizona Bulletin No. 9, Tucson, 1945.

Shipley, Joseph T., *Dictionary of World Literature.* "Folklore" by Stith Thompson, and other articles.* Philosophical Library, N. Y., 1943.

Taylor, Archer, *et. al.,* "A Platform," *California Folklore Quarterly,* I, January, 1942.

Texas Folklore Society Publications. Texas Folklore Society, Austin, and the University Press in Dallas, Annual volumes, I +, 1916 +.

Thompson, Stith, *Motif-Index of Folk-Literature,* 6 vols. Folklore Fellows Communication, Helsinki, and *Indiana University Studies,* Bloomington, Indiana, 1932-36.

Readers' Guide to Periodical Literature and *International Index to Periodicals,* H. W. Wilson Company, monthly and cumulated; and files of the following periodicals: *Journal of American Folklore,* American Folklore Society, University of Pennsylvania, 1888 +; *American Speech,* Columbia U. Press, 1925 +; *Southern Folklore Quarterly,* University of Florida, 1937 +; *Western Folklore* (formerly, *California Folklore Quarterly*), University of California Press, 1942 +; *Hoosier Folklore,* Indianapolis, Indiana, 1942 +; *New York Folklore Quarterly,* Cornell University Press, Ithaca, N. Y., 1945 +.

*The works marked with an asterisk should be read as preparation for research and collecting.

5

Suggestions for Further Study and for Collecting

1. Compare the definitions of *folklore* in various dictionaries and list the common elements.
2. Trace the history of collecting and folklore study in England, Germany and other European countries.
3. Analyze the relationships of the science of folklore to anthropology, sociology, and history.
4. Examine several copies of the folklore journals published in the United States and characterize each.
5. What subjects have been treated in the *Texas Folklore Society Publications,* or in the *Memoirs of the American Folklore Society?*
6. What kinds of material are included in Botkin's *A Treasury of American Folklore* and what sources does he list in the footnotes?
7. Try to divide into two lists your store of knowledge and your skills, using the headings "What I Learned in School" and "What I Picked Up from Other Folks."
8. Keep a clipping file of all folk materials that appear in newspapers and current magazines. Note the folk elements in radio programs, comic strips, etc.
9. Interview those who are likely to have memories full of folklore—old men and women, children, rural people and those not overly-educated.
10. Justify your study of folklore as a part of your own liberal education. How does it supplement your other studies?

CHAPTER TWO

FOLKLORE IN AMERICAN LIFE

Definitions and Comments

Racial or linguistic groupings of the inhabitants of various parts of the Western Hemisphere provide the basis for many folklore studies. Anthropologists have long been interested in the recording and the study of the native lore of the various Indian tribes. The literary folklorist may profitably consult their publications and compare the English translations of Indian myths and legends, songs and tales, beliefs and customs to those of European peoples. The Spanish, French, German and other foreign-language settlers in the new world brought with them much folklore, some of which survived in the new land. Foreign-language groups often continued to develop folklore of their own, as well as borrowing much from their neighbors. Attention to the folklore of various minority groups in the United States, including the Negro, should promote better inter-cultural understanding and add variety to our American heritage.

Regional influences are apparent in the different versions of common folk materials to be found in the different parts of the United States and of the other Western republics. New England, the Southwest, the Deep South, the Far West, etc., have, also, peculiar kinds of folklore that reflect the history, the population, and the physical environment of each specific region. The unique aspects

8

of regional cultures should be preserved as counterbalances to monotonous standardization.

Folklore in the United States may be studied profitably by means of other classifications than regional or linguistic differences. Groups may be based upon rural or urban localities, age levels, vocations, or social strata. Although folklore is often collected and published according to types, its place in social life becomes clearer if all of the folklore of a certain group is assembled and then compared to that of other groups.

Historians and other interpreters of American life are turning more and more to a study of our folklore in order to find the basic attitudes and ideologies that have dominated the masses of people at different periods in our national development. They are studying such popular symbols as folk heroes and such potent words and phrases as "the Western frontier," "manifest destiny," "free land," "business success," and "the common man." American literary historians now trace the evidences of folk sources and of folk materials in the works of Mark Twain, Melville, Hawthorne, and other masters.

Students of American art and music are becoming more and more aware of the rich contributions that anonymous folk artists and musicians have made; many new compositions are based upon or inspired by the creations of forgotten folk. There are countless revivals of old customs, crafts, folk arts, entertainments, and festivals. Evidently the folklore derived from earlier periods in United States history and the folk customs and arts borrowed from emigrant groups as well as from "native inhabitants" are functioning today in our attempts to understand and to perpetuate American culture.

9

Basic Readings* and General References

Anuario de la Sociedad Folklorica de Mexico. e.g., v. 6, 1945. Mexico, D.F., 1947.

Astrov, Margot, *The Winged Serpent: An Anthology of American Indian Prose and Poetry.* John Day Company, New York, 1946.

Ausubel, Nathan, *A Treasury of Jewish Folklore.* Crown, New York, 1948.

Barbeau, Marius, "French Folklore," in *Standard Dictionary of Folklore, Mythology, and Legend.* V. 1, pp. 416-425, Funk and Wagnalls, New York, 1949.

Boggs, Ralph S., *Bibliografia del Folklore Mexicano.* Instituto Paramericano de Geographia and Historia, Mexico, D. F., 1939.

Botkin, Ben A., *A Treasury of New England Folklore.** Crown, New York, 1947.

----------------------, *Folk-say: A Regional Miscellany.* Vols. I-IV, University of Oklahoma Press, Norman, 1929-32.

----------------------, *Lay My Burden Down: A Folk History of Slavery.* University of Chicago Press, Chicago, 1945.

----------------------, *A Treasury of Southern Folklore.** Crown, New York, 1949.

Bureau of American Ethnology, *Annual Reports* and *Bulletins,* Washington, D. C., 1881 +.

Campa, Arthur L., *Spanish Folk-Poetry in New Mexico.* University of New Mexico Press, Albuquerque, 1946.

"Canadian Number" of *Journal of American Folklore.* 63, April-June, 1950.

Curtis, Natalie, *The Indians' Book.** Harpers, New York, 1907.

Dorson, Richard M., *America Begins: Early American Writings.* Pantheon, New York, 1950.

Dobie, J. Frank, *Puro Mexicano*. Texas Folk-Lore Society Publication, XII, Austin, 1935.

Gardener, Evelyn E., *Folklore from the Schoharie Hills, New York*. Ann Arbor, Michigan, 1937.

Hodge, Frederick W., *Handbook of American Indians North of Mexico*. 2 v., Bureau of American Ethnology, Washington, D. C., 1907-10.

Hudson, Arthur Palmer, *Humor of the Old Deep South*. Macmillan, New York, 1931.

Onis, Harriet de, *The Golden Land: An Anthology of Latin American Folklore in Literature*. Knopf, New York, 1948.

Randolph, Vance, *Ozark Mountain Folks*.* The Vanguard Press, New York, 1932.

Saxon, Lyle; Dreyer, Edward; and Tallant, Robert, *Gumbo Ya-Ya*. Houghton Mifflin, Boston, 1945.

Spiller, Robert E., and others, *Literary History of the United States* (chapters on folklore and American humor). Macmillan, New York, 1948.

Stegner, Wallace, *Mormon Country*. Duell, Sloan and Pearce, New York, 1942.

Thompson, Harold W., *Body, Boots, and Britches*.* J. B. Lippincott, Philadelphia, 1940.

Toor, Frances, *A Treasury of Mexican Folkways*.* Crown, New York, 1947.

Waterman, Richard A. and Bascom, William R., "African and New World Negro Folklore," in *Standard Dictionary of Folklore, Mythology, and Legend*. v.1, pp. 18-24, 1949.

cf. the various regional folklore periodicals, e.g., *New York Folklore Quarterly, Hoosier Folklore*, the Daughters of Utah Pioneers pamphlets, *Tennessee Folklore Society*

Bulletin, New Mexico Folklore Record, North Carolina Folklore; magazines of the state and local historical societies; and the state guides prepared by the W.P.A.

Suggestions for Further Study and for Collecting

1. What has the Negro contributed to American folklore? What, the Spanish? What, the French?

2. How does the folklore of the South differ from that of New England or the Pacific coast?

3. Study the folklore of the Scandinavians, the Polish, the Chinese, or some other groups of foreign origin now living in an American community. What have they retained and what have they lost of their old-world cultural heritage?

4. How have the historical and the physical backgrounds of life in the Rocky Mountains entered into the folklore of that region?

5. What elements of Anglo-Saxon culture survive in the Ozarks or the mountains of Tennessee?

6. What folklore did the Irish bring to America? The Pennsylvania Germans? The English, Scotch, and Welsh?

7. Study the folklore of one vocation such as mining, lumbering, railroading, the cattle industry, the oil fields, automobile manufacturing, the army, carpentry, law, public school work, shipping, sugar beet industry, farming, or plumbing.

8. What lore is associated with the desert, mountains, forests, or rivers?

9. Study the lore connected with the Mormons, the Shakers, or some other religious sect.

10. Analyze the folk elements in the work of some American composer, author, or painter.

CHAPTER THREE

MYTHS, LEGENDS, AND TRADITIONS

Definitions and Comments

Myths are the stories of the gods and other supernatural beings. Usually in prose, they explain natural phenomena; often they parallel the religions of advanced cultures, forming the basis of the individual's adjustment to his universe and the unseen powers in it. In America different Indian tribes had their own bodies of myths, with common characteristics but varying in response to a tribe's peculiar environment and history.

Legends are stories of what supposedly took place in earlier times. They parallel history on the learned level. Many are associated with places; those attached to persons will be studied in the section devoted to "folk heroes." Legends and traditions constitute popular history, although usually containing more fiction than fact.

Traditions are the inherited explanations, attitudes, and responses orally transmitted as a part of folk education. They may concern events, objects, people, places, or behavior patterns.

Myths may be subdivided into such classifications as origin myths, ritual myths, incidents involving the lives of the gods, stories of culture heroes, trickster tales, journeys to the other world, human and animal marriages, adaptations of old world myths, and retellings of biblical stories.

14

Legends and traditions may be grouped under the following headings: place legends, saints' legends, miracle stories, buried treasure legends, stories of natural wonders or extraordinary places, migration legends, stories of sacred objects, tales of legendary characters, stories of ghosts, witches, devils, vampires, ogres, and haunted houses, accounts of transformation and supernatural appearances, and accounts of mythical animals. Those dealing with witchcraft and the return to earth of the spirits of the dead will be discussed under "Beliefs in the Supernatural."

Basic Readings* and General References

Alexander, Hartley B., *North American Mythology*, V. 10 of *The Mythology of All Races*, Marshall Jones Company, Boston, 1916; and *The Mythology of Latin American Races*, V. 11 of same.

Applegate, Frank G., *Indian Stories from the Pueblos*. J. B. Lippincott, Philadelphia, 1929.

Boas, Franz, *Tsimshian Mythology. Report of the Bureau of American Ethnology No. 31*, Washington, 1916.

Cushing, Frank, *Zuni Folk Tales.** Knopf, New York, 1901.

Dobie, J. Frank, *Coronado's Children.** Southwest Press, Dallas, 1930; *Apache Gold and Yaqui Silver*. Little, Brown, Boston, 1939.

Gerould, Gordon H., *Saints' Legends*. Houghton Mifflin, Boston, 1916.

Hallenbeck, Cleve and Williams, Juanita H., *Legends of the Spanish Southwest*. Arthur H. Clark, Glendale, California, 1938.

Janvier, Thomas A., *Legends of the City of Mexico*. Harper and Brothers, New York, 1910.

Linderman, Frank B., *Indian Old-Man Stories*. Scribners, New York, 1920.

Lummis, Charles F., *Pueblo Indian Folk-Stories*. Scribners, New York, 1910.

Matthews, Washington, *Navaho Legends*, V. 5 of the *Memoirs of the American Folklore Society*. Houghton Mifflin, Boston, 1897.

Reichar, Gladys A., *An Analysis of Coeur D'Alene Indian Myths*. V. 41 of the *Memoirs of the American Folklore Society*, Philadelphia, 1947.

Shoemaker, Henry W., *Some Stories of Old Deserted Houses from Central Pennsylvania.* Pennsylvania Folklore Society Publications, Altoona, 1931.

Skinner, Charles M., *Myths and Legends of Our Own Land.** 2 V., J. B. Lippincott, Philadelphia, 1896; *American Myths and Legends.** 2 V., Philadelphia, 1903.

Thompson, Stith, *Tales of the North American Indians.** Harvard University Press, Cambridge, Mass., 1929.

Wood, Charles E. S., *A Book of Indian Tales.* Vanguard Press, New York, 1929.

cf. the collections of myths published in the folklore journals, the *American Anthropologist,* the anthropological series of various universities, the bulletins and reports of the U. S. Bureau of Ethnology and other research organizations. See also the general folklore collections and the anthologies of children's literature.

Suggestions for Further Study and for Collecting

1. Collect the legends concerning the Revolutionary War, the Civil War, or World War II.

2. What legends are associated with the Alamo, Custer's Last Stand, the Oklahoma land rush in 1889, the Chicago fire, the San Francisco earthquake, the Gold Rush to California, the terrible winter of '89 or other important historical events?

3. What old world myths are told in America—from the Greek, the Scandinavian, the Germanic?

4. How do the myths of different Indian tribes resemble each other and how do they differ? What effect has Christianity had upon American Indian mythology?

5. What miracles are celebrated in American lore? Are there shrines of American saints?

6. What traditions are associated with Boston, New York, Washington, D. C., and other cities of the Western Hemisphere?

7. Collect the legends that have grown up around famous natural features, such as Niagara Falls, the Grand Canyon, stone faces or other forms in the mountains, and "starved rocks" or "lovers' leaps."

8. What stories are told about caves? Rivers? Lakes?

9. Find out all you can concerning buried treasure in your locality. What factual basis is there for the stories?

10. Collect all the stories that you can find about local crimes, disasters, great events, graveyards, founding of schools and churches, prominent families, haunted houses.

CHAPTER FOUR

FOLKTALES AND ANECDOTES

Definitions and Comments

Folktales are the secular, non-religious fictional narratives or short stories that circulate orally, illustrating the nature of everyday life or recounting the unusual, with entertainment the primary purpose. An emphasis upon what happens rather than upon character portrayal or descriptive detail characterizes the folktale. One tale often leads to another at a storytelling session. Taken together, they reveal much concerning the customs and attitudes of the group in which they circulate.

Nursery tales are stories that appeal especially to children. They often make use of the supernatural, the fearful, the wonderful, and the unexpected.

Animal fables may be told to illustrate a point, using animals in place of human participants; but the animals behave like people. Aesop's fables and Uncle Remus stories are well-known in the United States although they originated elsewhere.

Jests and humorous stories have always been popular in America. Sometimes they are told about Irishmen, Dutchmen, Negroes, Jews, mothers-in-law, brides, misers, greenhorns, or some other class of mortals whose behavior is held up for humorous or satirical attention.

Fairy tales are artistically developed narratives about super-human creatures that produce wonderful changes in the lives of the people who meet them. They differ from legends and traditional tales since they are told for amusement only. Many from the collections of the Grimm brothers in Germany, Hans Christian Anderson in Denmark, and Charles Perrault in France are known in the United States.

Tall tales thrive in the United States. Based upon reality they exaggerate until they pass all of the limits of plausibility, but they are told as if the narrator were prepared to swear to their truthfulness. Often rambling and seemingly pointless, they are usually the product of skillful storytelling techniques. Some of the best originated on the southern and western frontiers.

Queer tales often entertain the listener by arousing his fear of the unaccountable manifestations of the devil, of spirits of the dead, or of witches. Phantom ships, mysterious warnings, haunted houses are involved in many traditional tales.

One type of humorous anecdote is based upon strange and peculiar variations from normal nature. Animals are described that never existed; snakes behave with uncanny wisdom; the weather surpasses anything yet witnessed by man. The narrator's imagination runs wild, but he lies like the truth.

Another source of humor is the noodle or numbskull, now called the moron. His misadventures appear in innumerable anecdotes. Practical jokes played upon the unsuspecting novice also furnish materials for entertaining stories.

Much study of folktales has been made since Jakob and Wilhelm Grimm published their *Kinder-und Hansmarchen* in 1812-15 (translated into English as *House-*

hold Tales, 1884). The historic-geographic method recognizes the principle that many tales have been borrowed from one culture by another and have undergone various changes in this process and, also, in the retellings during successive ages. In order to trace borrowings and variants, the component elements in a tale are isolated and their distribution is traced through collections of tales made in different countries, languages, and periods. Thus a basic or original form may be approximated, the place and date of origin may be more closely arrived at, and the extent of the circulation of the "motif" or story unit may be studied.

The beginning student, however, should first become familiar with standard collections of folktales in print. Then, he would do well to listen as often as possible to storytellers who narrate informally what they have unconsciously accumulated in their memories during numerous storytelling sessions in the past. Thus he would come to understand the common types of oral narrative, the influence of a given narrator and his audience upon a theme, plot or motif, and the ways in which storytelling fits into common life. An analysis of the stylistic methods of different narrators might reveal much concerning the basis of literary artistry.

Basic Readings* and General References

Aarne, Antti and Thompson, Stith, *The Types of the Folk Tale*. Helsinki, 1927 and Edwards Brothers, Ann Arbor, Michigan, 1940.

Aswell, James R. et.al., *God Bless the Devil! Liars' Bench Tales*. University of North Carolina Press, Chapel Hill, North Carolina, 1940.

Boatright, Mody C., *Tall Tales of the Texas Cow Camps*. The Southwest Press, Dallas, 1934; and *Folk Laughter on the American Frontier*, Macmillan, New York, 1949.

Botkin, Ben A., editor, *Folk-Say, A Regional Miscellany*. 4 v., University of Oklahoma Press, Norman, Oklahoma, 1929-32.

Carmer, Carl, *The Hurricane's Children*. Farrar and Rinehart, New York, 1937.

Carriere, Joseph M., *Tales from the French Folk-Lore of Missouri*. Northwestern University, Evanston, Illinois, 1937.

Chase, Richard, *The Jack Tales*. Houghton Mifflin, Boston, 1943.

Clough, Ben C., *The American Imagination at Work*. Knopf, New York, 1947.

Davidson, Levette J., and Blake, Forrester, *Rocky Mountain Tales*. University of Oklahoma Press, Norman, Oklahoma, 1947.

Dorson, Richard M., *Jonathan Draws the Long Bow: New England Popular Tales and Legends*. Harvard University Press, Cambridge, Mass., 1946; and *America Begins*. Pantheon, New York, 1950.

Espinosa, José Manuel, *Spanish Folk-Tales from New*

Mexico. Memoir 30, American Folklore Society, New York, 1937.

Field, Rachel, *American Folk and Fairy Tales.* Scribners, New York, 1929.

Fortier, Alcee, *Louisana Folk Tales*, V.2 of *Memoirs of the American Folklore Society,* Houghton Mifflin, Boston, 1895.

Harris, Joel Chandler, *Nights with Uncle Remus.** Century, New York, 1881 and Houghton Mifflin, Boston, 1911; *Uncle Remus and His Friends.* Boston, 1892; *Uncle Remus, His Songs and His Sayings.* Appleton-Century, New York, 1880 and 1934.

Hudson, Arthur P., *Humor of the Old Deep South.* Macmillan, New York, 1936.

Hurston, Zora Neale, *Mules and Men.* J. B. Lippincott, Philadelphia, 1935.

Johnson, Edna, and Scott, Carrie E., *Anthology of Children's Literature.** Houghton Mifflin, Boston, 1935.

Komroff, Manuel, *The Great Fables of all Nations.* The Dial Press, New York, 1928.

Lee, F. H., *Folk Tales of All Nations.** Coward-McCann, New York, 1930.

Masterson, James R., *Tall Tales of Arkansaw.* Chapman and Grimes, Boston, 1942.

Meine, Franklin J., *Tall Tales of the Southwest.** Knopf, New York, 1930.

Publications of the Texas Folk-Lore Society. University Press in Dallas, Austin, etc., 1916 +. e.g. Volume 22, 1948, *The Sky Is My Tipi,* edited by Mody C. Boatright.

Thomas, Lowell, *Tall Stories.** Funk and Wagnalls, New York, 1946.

23

Thompson, Stith, *The Folktale.** The Dryden Press, New York, 1946.

—————————, *Motif-Index of Folk-Literature*, 6 vols., Helsinki and University of Indiana, Bloomington, Indiana, 1932-36.

Suggestions for Further Study and for Collecting

1. How many of Aesop's fables did you learn by hear-say? Do you know other fables? Can you trace any of them back to La Fontaine, or to India?

2. Compare the Uncle Remus Stories to the Reynard the Fox beast epic of medieval Europe. What other animal tales have been popular in America?

3. Collect stylistic traits of folktales. How many tales use the formula "Once upon a time" or "They lived happily ever after"?

4. How have old world fairy tales been modified for American children? Which ones have been adapted for stage, radio, motion pictures, comics, etc.?

5. Show how certain elements or *motifs* appear in different combinations in different tales.

6. What have been the favorite types of "lies" among fishermen and hunters? How many can be traced back to Baron Münchausen?

7. How have travelers' tales exaggerated the wonders of remote lands? What patterns of adventure reappear?

8. Analyze the jokes concerning minority groups or races and see how much they are based upon fact, how much on imagined characteristics?

9. What types of stories have been especially popular with children? At what ages do they outgrow these preferences? What types do they then desire?

10. Collect the wonder stories of your locality—those about big storms, clever animals, queer happenings, buried treasure, large crops, etc.

CHAPTER FIVE

FOLK HEROES

Definitions and Comments

Folk heroes may be classified as patriotic figures, frontiersmen, badmen, supermen, occupational heroes, and local characters.

Some historical figures have become the subject of popular legend—Washington, Franklin, Lincoln, Robert E. Lee, Ulysses S. Grant, Andrew Jackson, Boone, Crockett; but many American heroes have been created by the folk imagination. The latter figures usually illustrate such qualities of strength, skill, and daring as lead to success in everyday life; folk heroes possess these attributes to a superlative degree. Glorification sometimes results in comedy, as with Davy Crockett, Mike Fink, Paul Bunyan, Pecos Bill, Big-Foot Wallace and Slappy Hooper.

Although a folk hero may have emerged from actual historical events, he usually ended by becoming a popular symbol. Captain John Smith, Henry Hudson, Peter Stuyvesant, Miles Standish, Pocahontas, Roger Williams, Paul Revere, Nathan Hale, Ethan Allen, John Paul Jones, John Brown, Molly Pitcher, Barbara Frietchie, Brigham Young, Marcus Whitman, General Custer, and numerous others have entered the American Valhalla of patriots around whom legends cluster. Such recent figures as Theodore Roosevelt, William Jennings Bryan, Woodrow Wilson, Calvin Coolidge, Franklin D. Roosevelt, Eleanor

Roosevelt, and Dwight D. Eisenhower are told about in orally circulated, popular stories that, whether true or not, illustrate their personalities and the times in which they served our nation.

The good worker and the malefactor both stand out from the common run of men. Among the former were Johnny Appleseed, Buffalo Bill, John Henry, and Kit Carson; among the latter, Jesse James, Billy the Kid, Sam Bass, Dillinger, Cattle Kate, Pancho Villa, and Belle Starr. Much of the work of building our nation has been done by anonymous laborers who have been slightingly or humorously represented by such typical figures as the Irish Paddy, Ching, Ching Chinaman, John Henry, Pecos Bill, Casey Jones, the Pullman car porter George, the Wop, the Forty-niner, the bull whacker, the Doughboy, and the Oakie. Crime has always attracted attention. On the frontier it was sometimes difficult to differentiate between outlaws and sheriffs; both had to be trigger-men. Stories of famous shootings occupy a prominent place in the American hero tradition.

Representative figures from different regions serve as magnets for stories that show folk admiration or disapproval, e.g. the Yankee, the New England Puritan, the Pilgrim Father, the Connecticut Peddler, the Pike, the Southern Colonel, the Hoosier, the Cracker, the Hill-Billy, and the Oakie. Father Knickerbocker and the Philadelphia Quaker are examples of symbolic characters used, like Uncle Sam, by cartoonists and editorial writers.

Every locality has its distinguished citizens and its queer characters about whom gossip has woven elaborate legends. People who are extremely wealthy, who are hermits, who have a mysterious past, whose eccentricities are laughable, or who have distinguished themselves in some other way, add to the variety and the entertainment of the community. If not heroic, they are at least memorable.

Many well-known, popular, folk-like figures of today are to be found in newspaper comic strips, radio programs, and motion pictures. Although the product of individual creation and of commercial exploitation, such characters often pass into the folk tradition and continue to develop independently of their inventors. Frequently they were derived from folk materials and their authors draw upon folklore for the actions, speech, customs, dress, etc., that have proven attractive. The motion picture cowboy, cattle rustler, sheriff, and badman; the radio's Negro cronies "Amos and Andy"; and the comic strip's "Little Abner" or "Superman" are examples. Some high schools and colleges have even celebrated "Sadie Hawkins Day" with more enthusiasm than Washington's Birthday. The Lone Ranger, Mickey Mouse, Donald Duck, and Popeye are now almost as much a part of childhood as are Mother Goose characters.

Basic Readings* and General References

Abbott, John S. C., *Daniel Boone: the Pioneer of Kentucky.* Dodd, Mead, New York, 1872.

Alter, J. C., *James Bridger.* Shepard Book Company, Salt Lake City, 1929 (out of print).

Beath, Paul R., *Febold Feboldson: Tall Tales from the Great Plains.* University of Nebraska Press, Lincoln, Nebraska, 1948.

Blair, Walter, and Meine, Franklin J., *Mike Fink: King of Mississippi Keelboatmen.* Henry Holt, New York, 1933.

Blair, Walter, *Tall Tale America, A Legendary History of Our Humorous Heroes.** Coward-McCann, New York, 1944.

Boatright, Mody C., *Gib Morgan: Minstrel of the Oil Fields.* Texas Folk-Lore Society Publications, 20, El Paso, 1945.

Bowman, James C., *Pecos Bill: the Greatest Cowboy of All Time.* Whitman, Chicago, 1937.

Bradford, Roark, *John Henry.* Harper Brothers, New York, 1931.

Burns, Walter Noble, *The Saga of Billy the Kid.* Doubleday, Page, Garden City, New York, 1925.

Cody, William F., *An Autobiography of Buffalo Bill.* Cosmopolitan Book Corporation, New York, 1920.

Crockett, David, *The Autobiography of David Crockett.* "With an Introduction by Hamlin Garland." Scribners, New York, 1923.

Daugherty, James H., *Their Weight in Wildcats.* Houghton Mifflin, Boston, 1936.

Davidson, Levette J. and Blake, Forrester, *Rocky Mountain Tales* (cf. Jim Bridger and Sergeant O'Keefe).

29

University of Oklahoma Press, Norman, 1947.

Dorson, Richard M., *Davy Crockett, American Comic Legend*. Rockland Editions, New York, 1939.

............, ..., *Jonathan Draws the Long Bow*. Harvard University Press, Cambridge, Mass., 1946.

Duval, John C., *The Adventures of Big-Foot Wallace*. 1870. Reprint edition, Tardy Publishing Company, Dallas, 1936.

Felton, Howard W., *Legends of Paul Bunyan*. Knopf, New York, 1947.

Gard, Wayne, *Frontier Justice*. University of Oklahoma Press, Norman, 1949.

Holbrook, Stewart H., *Little Annie Oakley and Other Rugged People*. Macmillan, New York, 1948.

Ingraham, J. H., *Lafitte: the Pirate of the Gulf*. Pollard and Moss, New York, 1836.

Karsner, David, *Silver Dollar: The Story of the Tabors*. Covici, Friede, New York, 1932.

Jagendorf, Moritz, *The Marvelous Adventures of John Caesar Cicero Darling*. Vanguard Press, New York, 1949.

Lewis, Lloyd, *Myths After Lincoln*. Readers' Club Press, New York, 1941.

Raine, William M., *Famous Sheriffs and Western Outlaws*.* Garden City Publishing Company, Garden City, N. Y., 1929.

Rourke, Constance, *Davy Crockett*. Harcourt, Brace, New York, 1934.

Sandburg, Carl, *Abraham Lincoln: the Prairie Years*. Harcourt, Brace, New York, 1926.

Saxon, Lyle, *Lafitte the Pirate*. Century, New York, 1930.

Shay, Frank, *Here's Audacity! American Legendary Heroes.** Macaulay, New York, 1930.

Shepard, Esther, *Paul Bunyan.* McNeil Press, Seattle, Washington, 1925.

Sonnichsen, C. L., *Roy Bean, Law West of the Pecos.* Macmillan, New York, 1943.

Stevens, James, *Paul Bunyan.* Knopf, New York, 1925.

Vestal, Stanley, *Kit Carson: the Happy Warrior of the Old West.* Houghton Mifflin, Boston, 1928.

Wecter, Dixon, *The Hero in America.** Scribners, New York, 1941.

Waugh, Coulton, *The Comics.* Macmillan, New York, 1947.

Suggestions for Further Study and for Collecting

1. Try to separate fact from fiction in the books about one of the following: Buffalo Bill, Sacajawea, George Washington, Paul Revere, Judge Roy Bean, Kit Carson, Daniel Boone, Davy Crockett, Abraham Lincoln, Mike Fink and Jim Bridger.

2. Gather as many stories as you can find, in print and by interviewing old timers, concerning well-known local characters or famous people in your home town or state. Are there hermit stories, stories of queer people, of champion liars, of strong men, of shrews, of drunks, of misers?

3. Analyze the common characteristics of American folk heroes and contrast them to the qualities admired in the heroes of other cultures.

4. How have the heroes of one period differed from those of a different period? Who are our heroes of today?

5. What outstanding traits are present in the heroes of Indian lore?

6. List America's great occupational heroes, such as Paul Bunyan; then find out how much information concerning a given occupation is woven into the stories concerning one representative figure.

7. How and why have such outlaws as Jesse James, Billy the Kid, and Soapy Smith become folk heroes?

8. Who are the heroes and who the villains of the Hollywood movie, the comic strip, the radio dramas, and popular fiction? How do they differ from the early popular characters of oral tradition?

9. Compare the different folk and literary versions of the life of Johnny Appleseed, Casey Jones, John

Henry, Big-Foot Wallace, Sam Bass, Quantrell, Wild Bill Hickok, and Calamity Jane.

10. What legends are attached to John Smith, John Brown, Benjamin Franklin, and other national figures?

CHAPTER SIX

SONGS, BALLADS, AND RHYMES

Definitions and Comments

In the oral tradition various poetic devices such as meter, stanzaic form, and rhyme have aided the memory and have added beauty to folk expressions. Folk poetry includes story-telling ballads; emotionally expressive songs; amusing rhymes of childhood; word formulas such as street cries, prayers, graces and epitaphs; and familiar verses that are often-quoted but of forgotten authorship.

Songs that tell a story or portray an incident are called ballads. Those that have had a long existence are usually called *traditional,* such as the ones collected by Francis J. Child in his famous *English and Scottish Popular Ballads.* Some from this collection, as well as other old world ballads from across the seas, have been found still circulating orally in various parts of the new world. More recent ballads have told of train wrecks, of heroes, of crimes, of personal adventures, and of historical events. The newspaper and the radio have largely crowded out this type.

Lyrical songs may treat of love, or sorrow, or some other emotion. From ancient times lullabies have been used to quiet babies; and the singing of carols, many of them traditional, is a universal Christmas custom. Comic songs are enjoyed by groups of all ages. Songs from the aristocratic tradition or from the music hall were sometimes absorbed into the folk heritage; for example, some of Stephen Foster's.

Work songs have been collected from cowboys, miners, sailors, section hands, stevedores, cotton choppers. They reflect the conditions of labor and, also, common human attitudes. Often one worker will sing a stanza and then all will join in on the chorus, performing in rhythm to the song such cooperative tasks as hoisting an anchor, picking cotton, or laying rails.

Nearly every section of America and every historical period, as well as every folk vocation, including that of the hobo, has contributed its share to "the American Songbag." A few soldier songs have emerged from every war; and songs that once cheered the pioneers along the overland trails are still enjoyed. Even the homesteaders sang while "starving to death on a government claim." More recently folk singing has been used in labor unions and in social protest circles, with Casey Jones dying because he took his train out during a strike. Although tastes change somewhat from generation to generation, sentimental songs are always popular. Today, radio artists often feature "heart ballads," mingling survivals from "the gay nineties" with the latest creations of "tin-pan alley."

The songs and rhymes of children include those used for rope-jumping, counting out, and other games. Charms, taunts and challenges have taken verse form. Sentimental rhymes reappear over and over again in memory books. Even learning is aided by jingles, such as the one about the number of days in each month. Most prayers and graces known by children are traditional and in verse.

Religious songs may be in the learned or the folk

tradition. Among the most beautiful are the spirituals of the southern Negro. There are, also, Negro songs of protest and Negro "blues." At old-fashioned religious revivals the congregations, whether white or black, would meet for several days of singing, praying, and preaching. The *Sacred Harp Hymnal,* using shaped notes, was popular for over a century.

Basic Readings* and General References

Beck, Earl C., *Songs of the Michigan Lumberjacks.* Ann Arbor, University of Michigan Press, 1941.

Belden, Henry M., *Ballads and Songs Collected by the Missouri Folklore Society.* University of Missouri, Columbia, Mo., 1940.

Black, Eleanora, and Robertson, Sidney, *The Gold Rush Song Book.* The Colt Press, San Francisco, 1941.

Boni, Margaret B., and Lloyd, Norman, *Fireside Book of Folk Songs.* Simon and Schuster, New York, 1947.

Carmer, Carl, *Songs of the Rivers of America.* Farrar and Rinehart, New York, 1942.

Chase, Richard, *Old Songs and Singing Games.* University of North Carolina Press, Chapel Hill, 1938.

Child, Francis J., *The English and Scottish Popular Ballads.* I Vol., edited by Sargent and Kittredge. Houghton Mifflin, Boston, 1904.

Colcord, Joanna C., *Songs of American Sailormen.* W. W. Norton, New York, 1938.

Collins, Fletcher, Jr., *Alamance Play Party Songs and Singing Games.* Elon College, North Carolina, 1940.

Davidson, Levette J., "Mormon Songs," *Journal of American Folklore,* LVIII (Oct.-Dec., 1945), pp. 273-300.

Dolph, Edward A., *Sound Off! Soldier Songs.* Farrar and Rinehart, New York, 1942.

Eddy, Mary O., *Ballads and Songs from Ohio.* J. J. Augustin, New York, 1931.

Fife, Austin E., and Alta, S., "Folk-Songs of Mormon Inspiration," *Western Folklore,* VI (Jan., 1947), pp. 42-52.

Finger, Charles J., *Frontier Ballads.* Doubleday, Garden City, New York, 1927.

Gordon, Robert W., *Folk-Songs of America*. In *New York Times*, 1927-28. Reprinted, W.P.A., 1938.

Hille, Waldemar, *The People's Song Book*. Boni and Gear, New York, 1948.

Jackson, George Pullen, *White and Negro Spirituals*. J. J. Augustin, New York, 1944.

――――――, ―――――― ――――――, *Down East Spirituals and Others*. J. J. Augustin, New York, 1943.

――――――, ―――――― ――――――, *The Story of the Sacred Harp*. Vanderbilt University Press, Nashville, 1944.

Johnson, James Weldon, and Rosamund, J., *The Book of American Negro Spirituals.** Viking, New York, 1940.

Kolb, Sylvia and John, *A Treasury of Folk Songs*. Bantam Books, New York, 1948.

Korson, George G., *Minstrels of the Mine Patch*. University of Pennsylvania Press, Philadelphia, 1938.

――――――, ――――――, *Coal Dust on the Fiddle*. University of Pennsylvania, Philadelphia, 1943.

Lomax, John and Alan, *Folk Song: U. S. A.** Duell, Sloan and Pearce, New York, 1947.

――――――, ――――――, *American Ballads and Folk Songs*. Macmillan, New York, 1938.

――――――, ――――――, *Negro Folk Songs as Sung by Lead Belly*. Macmillan, New York, 1936.

――――――, ――――――, *Our Singing Country*. Macmillan, New York, 1941.

――――――, ――――――, *Cowboy Songs and Other Frontier Ballads*. Revised. Macmillan, New York, 1938.

Larkin, Margaret, and Black, Helen, *Singing Cowboy*. Knopf, New York, 1931.

Luther, Frank, *Americans and Their Songs*. Harper Brothers, New York, 1942.

Newell, W. W., *Songs and Games of American Children.**
Harper Brothers, New York, 1884, 1903, 1911.

Niles, John Jacob, *Ballads, Carols and Tragic Legends.*
Schirmer, American Folk-Song Series, New York, 1938,
etc. (cf. others in Series).

Randolph, Vance, *Ozark Folksongs,* I-IV. Missouri State
Historical Society, Columbia, Missouri, 1946-1950.

Rickaby, Franz L., *Ballads and Songs of the Shantyboy.*
Harvard University Press, Cambridge, Mass., 1926.

Sandburg, Carl, *The American Songbag.** Harcourt,
Brace, New York, 1927.

Sharp, Cecil J., *English Folk Songs from the Southern
Appalachians.* 2V. Oxford University Press, London,
1932.

Shay, Frank, *My Pious Friends and Drunken Companions.*
Macauley, New York, 1927.

--------------, --------------------, *American Sea Songs.* Revised. W.
W. Norton, New York, 1948.

Wells, Evelyn Kendrick, *The Ballad Tree.** The Ronald
Press, New York, 1950.

Wheeler, Mary, *Steamboatin' Days: Folk Songs of the
River Packet Era.* Louisiana University Press, Baton
Rouge, 1944.

Withers, Carl, *A Rocket in My Pocket: the Rhymes and
Chants of Young Americans.* Henry Holt, 1948.

Suggestions for Further Study and for Collecting

1. List all the songs and ballads that you learned by listening to other people sing at their work or play. How many can you find in folklore collections? How do your versions differ from those in print?

2. Study the songs and ballads that have emerged from one industry or occupation—cattle industry, railroading, college life, prison camps. Show how the environment and the common experiences shaped the words and music used.

3. How do American Negro spirituals differ from the selections in the *Methodist Hymnal* or some other collection of religious songs?

4. Collect the verses that children repeat when trying to be smart, or insulting, or funny, or sentimental.

5. Study the traditional songs of some non-English speaking group in the United States—the Spanish-American, the French, the Polish. How many elements in them reflect the land of origin of the people or of the language?

6. Compare all the versions that you can find of "Barbara Allen" or some other traditional ballad. Which do you like best and why? How do the tunes differ?

7. What were the popular songs of the western frontier? of the '49'ers? of the Mormons?

8. What calls or cries have been used by street merchants or peddlers?

9. What lyrics and tunes have been borrowed from the Irish? the Welsh? the English?

10. What differentiates popular songs from folk songs? Do they ever change places? cf. "Oh, Susannah," "Irene," "Itiskit, Itasket," and "Home on the Range."

41

CHAPTER SEVEN

FOLK SPEECH AND FOLK SAYINGS

Definitions and Comments

Folk speech differs from "standard" speech in various ways: it retains some words and usages regarded as obsolete by authorities; it admits others that are ahead of the literary language; and it is flavored with localisms, slang, and sub-standard formulations. It gives a distinctive flavor to all verbal forms of folklore such as songs and tales, and to common daily speech.

Dialects are local or provincial patterns of speech, deviating more or less in pronunciation, syntax, vocabulary, etc., from the standard. In the "American language" regional variations are less strongly marked in their difference from "standard English" than dialects of other tongues, which may form distinct sub-languages. Yet, markedly different pronunciation patterns, varying influences of other languages upon "American"—as Spanish in the Southwest—, different coinages and the preservation of old, even archaic English forms, make the definition and study of American dialects a fascinating, difficult study which now requires both precision and delicacy.

Place names for towns, rivers, or mountains may be colorless or full of connotation. A study of their origins explains much about the folkways and the legends of a community. American place names, like those of other lands, are often derived from the names of famous people; and as often from the names of sometimes forgotten early settlers. Distinctively American is the borrowing and adaptation of Indian names. Names derived from incidents in early American history are sometimes picturesque or poetic, sometimes humorous or grim. Many names are transferred from other communities, and many are descriptive of near-by geographical features.

Special vocabularies are used by workers in various trades or professions: by criminals, cults or gangs. These include cant, jargon, lingo, argot. Much criminal cant has worked its way into popular, fashionable slang. Workers in the entertainment business and members of the armed services have rich special vocabularies which are renewed by the coining of colorful popular terms for technological developments. These special terminologies are not confined to "low life"; teachers, lawyers, doctors, and other professional men use words and expressions not generally known and in addition to the technical phraseology of their crafts.

Slang is made up of relatively new-terms used to enliven popular speech; it is ephemeral in nature and subliterary. However, some "slang" words do, in the course of centuries, rise to top-level, "formal" usage. Because most slang becomes quickly staled through usage and is replaced by new slang, a study of this kind of folk invention is an aid in interpreting the spirit of past decades. A surprising number of words and expressions now used as slang are to be found in early "classic" writings.

Proverbs are traditional formulations of folk wisdom, beliefs, and attitudes in brief sentences or phrases. Some are of learned origin, but now are current in popular speech. "A proverb is to speech what salt is to food." Many proverbs commonly used by the folk were derived from literature, and sometimes from the most revered writings. But literature has, in its turn, taken up with profit the proverbs evolved from folk wisdom and folk speech.

Riddles are verbal puzzles that say one thing and mean another; the hearer is to guess the answer although the clues given are phrased so as to mislead him. Riddles bandied about by children today are most often word-twisting; but some embody comment on current events. In the past, folk riddles were sometimes magic spells or runes; or, in cryptic form, they contained political satire and other bits of folk wisdom.

Smart sayings are a variety of folk humor phrased to illustrate the superior cleverness of the speaker, often to the chagrin of the listener if they are verbal tricks. Smart retorts are also cherished, especially by the young. "Wise cracks" come into fashion, become tiresome by repetition, pass from current usage and are indices to historical periods in the same way that slang is. Some smart sayings are folk-bandyings or epigrams and telling lines from poetry, oratory, and other literature.

Picturesque speech includes vivid metaphors and homely similes, symbolic terms, phrases borrowed from sports, unexpected contrasts, witty remarks. A related form, tall talk, is full of the self-importance of the speaker or of his pride in his origins, couched in purple passages of rhetoric, exaggeration and boasting. Formulas for such have become traditional.

American frontier tall talk attained expressiveness by making its "brags" in terms of specific and particular circumstances rather than in bombastic generalities. Mark Twain included good examples in *Life on the Mississippi*. The boasting phrase itself is a kind of compressed, heroic anecdote. Paralleling tall talk and serving the same purpose were phrases and tales of wry understatement. These twin devices had much to do with forming the character of American humorous writing as it appeared in newspapers of the advancing West and culminated in Mark Twain.

Honorifics, euphemisms, expletives include terms conferring honor or abuse, words substituted for vulgar or sacred expressions, and words or phrases that fill in, such as profanity. Examples in abundance may be found in everyday life.

Sign language is used where noise renders hearing difficult, where silence is needed, or where a spoken language would not be understood. Among the Plains Indians, folk-invented sign language became a wonderfully expressive means of communication between tribes using different languages. Sign languages for the deaf and dumb are representative of deliberately invented, non-folk signalling systems. Some sign systems used in trades have been invented, others have evolved in a "folk" process (cf. the signs of a train crew or of radio broadcasting). Individual signs or gestures are used as a substitute for speech or to accompany, reinforce, or fill in the gaps of oral language. Orators have long used formal systems of gesture for these purposes. Characteristic national and regional gestures are yet to be investigated fully by the folklorist; but folk gestures with well-known significance are used in all circles.

Other speech patterns on the folk or popular level are

45

"pig-Latin" and other secret languages, imitations of animal sounds and calls, toasts, compliments, mixtures of languages, Wellerisms, Spoonerisms, and forbidden words.

Folk etymologies are popular twistings of the pronunciation of words, of their syntactical forms, and of their use in combinations and in meanings; often these changes are illogical but expressive. Folk usage can also establish even the spelling of words; thus the folk help to determine "accepted forms."

Basic Readings* and General References

Adams, O. S., "Traditional Proverbs and Sayings from California." *Western Folklore,* VI (Jan., 1947), pp. 59-64.

――――, ――――, "More California Proverbs." *Western Folklore,* VII (April, 1948), pp. 136-144.

Adams, Ramon F., *Western Words: A Dictionary of the Range, Cow Camp and Trail.* University of Oklahoma Press, Norman, Oklahoma, 1944.

Berrey, Lester V., and Van den Bark, Melvin, *American Thesaurus of Slang.* Crowell, New York, 1942; with Supplement, 1947.

Bentley, Harold W., *A Dictionary of Spanish Terms in English.* Columbia University Press, New York, 1932.

Burke, W. J., *The Literature of Slang* (bibliography). New York Public Library, New York, 1939.

Caffee, N. M., and Kirby, T. S., eds., *Studies for William A. Read.* University of Louisiana Press, Baton Rouge, 1940.

Craigie, W. A., and Hulbert, James R., *A Dictionary of American English,* 4 Vols. University of Chicago Press, Chicago, 1936-1944.

Davidson, Levette J., "The Vocabulary of a Westerner." *Southwest Review,* XXIV (Oct., 1938), pp. 62-74.

――――, ――――, "Some Current Folk Gestures." *American Speech,* XXV (Feb., 1950), pp. 3-9.

Eikel, Fred, Jr., "Aggie Vocabulary of Slang." *American Speech,* XXI (Spring, 1946), pp. 29-36.

Espinosa, A. M., "California Spanish Folklore Riddles." *California Folklore Quarterly,* III (Oct., 1944), pp. 292-299.

Flanagan, John T., "Texas Speaks Texan." *Southwest Review*, XXXI (Spring, 1946), pp. 191-2.

Funk, Charles Earle, *A Hog on Ice*. Harpers, New York, 1948.

Garnett, Henry, *American Names*. Public Affairs Press, Washington, D. C., 1947.

Gudde, Erwin G., *California Place Names: A Geographical Dictionary*. University of California, Berkeley, 1949.

Hockett, Charles F., "Reactions to Indian Place Names." *American Speech*, XXV (May, 1950), pp. 118-121.

Johnson, Burges, *The Lost Art of Profanity*. Bobbs-Merrill, Indianapolis and New York, 1948.

Kittredge, George L., *The Old Farmer and His Almanac*. Harvard University Press, Cambridge, Mass., 1924.

Krapp, George P., *The English Language in America*,* 2 Vols. Century, New York, 1925.

Maurer, David W., *The Big Con*. Pocket Books, Inc., New York, 1949, and Bobbs-Merrill, Indianapolis, 1940.

Mencken, H. L., *The American Language*.* Knopf, New York, 1919, fourth edition, 1936; Supplement One, 1945; Supplement Two, 1948.

Pearce, Helen, "Folk Sayings in a Pioneer Family of Western Oregon." *California Folklore Quarterly*, V (July, 1946), pp. 229-242.

Pearce, Thomas N., "New Mexican Folk Etymologies." *El Palacio*, L (August, 1943), pp. 229-234.

Publications of the American Dialect Society. Sec.-Treas. of A.D.S., Greensboro, North Carolina, 1941 +.

Shafer, Robert, "Language of West Coast Culinary Workers." *American Speech*, XXI (April, 1946), pp. 86-89.

Shankle, G. E., *American Nicknames*. H. W. Wilson Co., New York, 1937.

Smith, Wm. G., etc., *The Oxford Dictionary of English Proverbs*. Oxford University Press, N. Y., (revised edition) 1948.

Stevenson, Burton, *The Home Book of Proverbs, Maxims and Familiar Phrases*. Macmillan, New York, 1948.

Stewart, George R., *Names on the Land; a Historical Account of Place-Naming in the United States*.* Random House, New York, 1945.

Sylvester, A. H., "Place-Naming in the Northwest." *American Speech*, XVIII (December, 1943), pp. 241-252.

Taylor, Archer, *The Proverb*.* Harvard University Press, Cambridge, Massachusetts, 1931.

------------, ---------------, *English Riddles from Oral Tradition*. University of California Press, Berkeley, announced for 1950.

Variety, news weekly for entertainment professions, New York and California editions.

Wentworth, Harold, *American Dialect Dictionary*. Crowell, New York, 1944.

Weseen, Maurice H., *A Dictionary of American Slang*. Crowell, New York, 1934.

Whiting, B. J., "Origins of the Proverb." *Harvard Studies and Notes in Philology and Literature*, XIII, pp. 47-80.

Woods, Henry F., *American Sayings: Famous Phrases, Slogans, and Aphorisms*. Essential Books, Duel, Sloan and Pearce, New York, 1945.

Zoff, Otto, *Riddles Around the World*. Pantheon, New York, 1945.

Cf., other articles in *American Speech* and the various regional folklore magazines.

Suggestions for Further Study and for Collecting

1. Attempt a collection of trade words or technical language peculiar to a group or occupation with which you are familiar.

2. Make a collection of dialect words peculiar to your own locality.

3. Look into the history of towns, rivers, mountains, lakes, and other natural features with which you are familiar or in which you are interested, to discover the origin of their names.

4. Watch for advertisements, editorials, chamber of commerce reports, or speeches which try to "boost" a state, community, or product. Does the art of *tall talk* still survive?

5. List some of the proverbs and proverbial expressions that you have heard. Check to see if they are in the proverb dictionaries.

6. Make a study of the slang current in your social circle. Where does it come from? Why is it used? How long does it last?

7. Study the differences between New England, southern and western speech — vocabularies, pronunciations, idioms, etc.

8. Collect the popular names for plants, animals, and other creatures. How do they differ from the scientific names?

9. List the smart sayings and the picturesque speech that you may hear during one week.

10. What are the signs used by the players and by the officials in various ball games?

11. What gestures have you observed used to accompany

speech, to fill in gaps of speech, or to take the place of speech?

12. What twistings of "standard" English words and their uses, and "standard" grammatical usage can you find: from the use of the uneducated, or in fairly common oral, if not written, use?

CHAPTER EIGHT

BELIEFS IN THE SUPERNATURAL

Definitions and Comments

Folk beliefs are those not sanctioned by the authority
of formal religions; they are usually called superstitions.
When supplanted by scientific knowledge, they linger
on as entertaining survivals of a less sophisticated way of
life.

Witchcraft is the opposite of the good white magic of
the church. Supernatural beings in league with the devil,
or humans who have gained supernatural power by black
magic, cause many wonders and much evil, according to
report. Everyone tries to avoid witches, unless he wants
them to foretell his future; but everyone has heard many
stories about them. Witch killing has not been popular
in the United States since the Salem trials in 1692, but
even today the newspapers occasionally report witchcraft
doings, and not just on Hallowe'en. Some folk tales
report appearances of the devil himself. Others tell how
evil people make effigies of enemies, and torture their
foes through mistreatment of the images. A few individuals are said to possess the evil eye.

Some witchcraft which survives among the relatively
uneducated sections of our population is thought of as an
aid to forecasting and to the procuring of success in en-
terprises of love and gambling. Objects needed for voodoo
conjuration—such as roots and candles—as well as books

53

on the interpretation of dreams and other omens, are sold in the shops of New York and other large cities. "Pulp" magazines frequently contain advertisements of these objects and of especially enchanting perfumes which are actually disguised love-philtres. Dream books are taken as an aid mainly by "policy" gamblers who are anxious to find magic (and winning) numbers. Fortune-telling by playing cards comes from ancient, medieval and Oriental ideas about the supernatural quality of the symbols on the cards.

Revenants, familiarly known as ghosts, are the restless spirits of the dead, who return to the haunts of their former existence for various reasons. Graveyards may be peopled, also, by ghouls and by vampires. Strange creatures such as fairies, gremlins, and Tommy-knockers are still talked about, but never seen.

Spiritualism and mediumship—designed to bring the dead back into communication with the living—are today religious and even commercial practices, historically connected with primitive shamanism and old magic. More common evidences of superstition are chain letters and chain prayers sent through the mails with instructions to the receiver to copy and send them on, or risk ill fortune by neglecting to do so. Various occupations have their folklore of superstitions, also, particularly when the workers are dependent on varying public favor—like actors—or on the perils of varying elements—like sailors.

Good luck and bad luck—how to gain the former and how to avoid the latter—have occupied the attention of countless folks. In the background lies the belief that our fate is controlled by unseen powers to whom certain objects and actions are propitiatory while others are offensive. The origins of some of our superstitions may be explained by reason; other beliefs are merely a part of our unquestioned folk heritage. Gamblers seem to possess many superstitions. So do most illiterate people. Is anyone entirely free from irrational beliefs?

Magical power is thought to reside in some objects, such as a horseshoe or a rabbit's foot for good luck, or a *charm*. There is a whole lore of the good and bad luck brought by different gems—as the good luck brought by one's own birthstone and the fortunate significance Indian tribes attribute to turquoise. Some actions and objects are *taboo*, such as walking on the opposite side of a tree from a companion. In this case, however, evil can be warded off by saying, "Bread and butter." Numbers, like 13, and days, like Friday, have a long-standing evil significance through folk belief. *Omens* indicate forthcoming events. Many people "knock on wood" to avoid an evil that they have just mentioned, such as sickness or accidents that they have previously missed; the wood is symbolic of the cross of Christ, although the connection may be forgotten.

Basic Readings* and General References

Barbeau, Marius, "Totemism, a Modern Growth on the North Pacific Coast," *Journal of American Folklore,* LVII, (Jan.-March, 1944), pp. 51-58.

Blaisdell, Elinore, *Tales of the Undead.* Crowell, New York, 1947.

Cannon, Mittamlin, "Angels and Spirits in Mormon Doctrine," *California Folklore Quarterly,* IV (Oct., 1945), pp. 343-350.

Carmer, Carl, *Stars Fell on Alabama.* Farrar and Rhinehart, New York, 1934.

DeLys, Claudia, *A Treasury of American Superstition.** Philosophical Library, New York, 1948.

Fate, Monthly Magazine, Evanston, Illinois.

Fielding, William J., *Strange Superstition and Magical Practices.* Blakiston Company, Philadelphia, 1945.

Frazer, Sir James G., *The Golden Bough,* one volume edition.* Macmillan, New York, 1922.

Hand, W. D., "Popular Beliefs and Superstitions from Oregon," *California Folklore Quarterly,* IV (Oct., 1945), pp. 427-432.

Hankey, Rosalie, "California Ghosts." *California Folklore Quarterly,* I (April, 1942), pp. 155-177.

Hark, Ann, *Hex Marks the Spot in the Pennsylvania Dutch Country.* Lippincott, New York, 1938.

Jones, Louis C., "Hitchhiking Ghosts in New York," *California Folklore Quarterly,* III (Oct., 1944), pp. 284-292.

------------, ---------------, *Spooks of the Valley.* Houghton Mifflin, Boston, 1948.

Kittredge, George L., *Witchcraft in Old and New Eng-*

land.* Harvard University Press, Cambridge, Mass., 1929.

Lee, Hector, *The Three Nephites.* University of New Mexico Press, Albuquerque, 1949.

Lowndes, M. S., *Ghosts That Still Walk: Real Ghosts of America.* Knopf, New York, 1941.

Lum, Peter, *The Stars in Our Heaven, Myths and Fables.* Pantheon, New York, 1948.

Mather, Cotton, *Magnalia Christi Americana (1620-1698).* Hartford, 1853.

Nichols, John N., "How to Become a Witch," *Tennessee Folklore Society Bulletin,* XVI, I, March, 1950, p. 14.

Radford, E. and M. A., *Encyclopedia of Superstition.* Philosophical Library, New York, 1949.

Randolph, Vance, *Ozark Superstitions.* Columbia University Press, New York, 1947.

Santschi, R. J., *Doodlebugs and Mysteries of Treasure Hunting.* Century Press, Oak Park, Illinois, 1941.

Tallant, Robert, *Voodoo in New Orleans.* Macmillan, New York, 1946.

Thomas, Daniel L. and Thomas B., *Kentucky Superstitions.* Princeton University Press, Princeton, N. J., 1930.

Underhill, Ruth M., *Singing for Power: the Song Magic of the Papago Indians of Southern Arizona.** University of California Press, Berkeley, California, 1938.

Waterman, Philip F., *The Story of Superstition.* Knopf, New York, 1929.

Yelvington, H., *Ghost Lore.* The Naylor Company, San Antonio, 1936.

Suggestions for Further Study and for Collecting

1. List ten ways to bring good luck and ten that will bring bad luck.

2. How do religious beliefs differ from superstitions? Cite examples.

3. Collect the ghost stories of your locality. Does anyone believe them?

4. Are there any haunted houses in your community? If so, how have the haunts behaved?

5. Have you ever heard of corpses coming back to life, or of people being buried before they were dead?

6. Study the witchcraft trials of Salem, Massachusetts, in 1692. What were the witches accused of doing?

7. What traits are ascribed to the devil in the stories that you have heard about him?

8. What does it mean to hear a dog howl at night, to drop the dishrag, for one's hand to itch, to take the last cake on the plate, etc.?

9. How can you have your wishes come true by lucky dealings with the wishbone of a chicken or by reciting a verse when you see the first star at night?

10. By what methods may one defend himself from evil spirits? from bad luck? from accidents while traveling?

CHAPTER NINE

FOLK WISDOM

Definitions and Comments

Folk wisdom preserves many directives that, if followed, are supposed to lead to success in the conduct of life. Some of this wisdom is summed up in proverbs, some is transmitted as custom. It is the substance of the informal instruction that one person enjoys passing on to another, especially to a younger one.

Various methods for foretelling the future, for discovering lost objects, for locating water or gold, and for reading character have been handed down from generation to generation. Some of this wisdom is possessed by special groups, e.g. fortune tellers, and is used professionally; some is widely distributed and freely given. Charlatans have prospered because they made a show of special knowledge and, often, of special equipment such as divining rods, phrenological charts, and mysterious crystal balls. These divining arts, although once founded on conceptions of the supernatural and on occult religions or philosophies, have taken on an extra-religious character in our century. Their apparently successful practice is often dependent on a shrewd, if unorganized and unwritten, knowledge of human psychology and behavior.

Astrology, interpreting characters and the future by the stars, was once inseparable from astronomy, the now scientific study of the physical universe beyond the earth.

The late Adolf Hitler, some movie stars, and even some figures in the worlds of business and of fashion designing, have in recent times been customers of astrologists, as were most of the world's leaders up to the 17th century. This commercialized use of the lore of the stars proceeds from pagan religions which maintained that the constellations are the forms of mythical beings, and from the philosophical notion, characteristic of neo-Platonism, that events on earth are a copy of, and have a correspondence to, designs in the heavens.

Another "fad" of our times has been the belief in numerology: that events can be foretold, wise courses be chosen, and propitious names or days be derived by studying number combinations. This pseudo-science stems from the magic of numbers and the belief of the ancient philosopher and mathematician Pythagoras that numbers are not mere representations but independent and powerful entities.

Long before the development of scientific medicine, and in many places and under many circumstances in more recent times, folk remedies and cures have been administered without professional aid for the relief of human sicknesses and suffering. Some were helpful; others, detrimental. Innumerable cures for warts, however, have been tried; but no sure cure has been established.

There is an extensive lore concerning plants, animals, perfumes, drugs, jewels, etc., that is not a part of the science of botany, zoology, or any other true science. Weather lore, especially, has always been prominent, if not dependable. How and when to plant, when to cultivate, and when to harvest have their answers in the lore of farming groups who never heard of scientific agriculture. The same type of situation exists for nearly every other human activity.

The persistence of the mythological instinct, or willingness to believe in fancied and wonderful animals and objects, can be observed in modern folk tales about sea-serpents, prehistoric monsters, men from Mars and flying saucers, as transmitted either by newspapers or orally. Occasionally, folk accounts of odd beings or happenings—of monsters, showers of fish and the like—are shown to have a determinable cause, almost as marvelous as the story which has grown up about it.

One might say that whatever we know, or think we know, that is not a part of the learning taught in schools, may be considered folk wisdom. Today, much of it is folly. Science proposes eventually to absorb all demonstrable truth.

Basic Readings* and General References

Aurand, Ammon Monroe, *Popular Home Remedies and Superstitions of the Pennsylvanian Germans.* Aurand Press, Harrisburg, Pennsylvania, 1941.

Bergen, Fanny D., *Animal and Plant Lore.* American Folklore Society, Boston, 1899.

Black, Pauline M., *Nebraska Folk Cures.* W.P.A. Pamphlets, Lincoln, Nebraska, 1940.

Clement, Ora A., *In All Its Fury: A History of the Blizzard of January 12, 1888.* Union College Press, Lincoln, Nebraska, 1947.

Curtin, L. S., *Healing Herbs of the Upper Rio Grande.* San Vincente Foundation, Santa Fe, N. M., 1947.

De Claremont, Lewis, *Legends of Incense, Herb and Oil Magic.* Dorene Publishing Company, New York, 1938.

Evans, Bergen, *The Natural History of Nonsense.* Knopf, New York, 1946.

Fort, Charles, *The Book of Charles Fort.* Holt, New York, 1941.

Haggard, Howard W., *Devils, Drugs, and Doctors.** Harper Brothers, New York, 1929.

Hering, Daniel W., *Foibles and Fallacies of Science.** D. Van Nostrand, New York, 1924.

Ingersoll, Ernest, *Birds in Legend, Fable and Folklore.* New York, 1923.

Johnson, Clifton, *What They Say in New England: A Book of Signs, Sayings, and Superstitions.* Lee and Shepard, Boston, 1896.

Jones, Louis C., "Practitioners of Folk Medicine," *Bulletin of the History of Medicine,* XXIII (Sept.-Oct., 1949), pp. 480-493.

Kittredge, George L., *The Old Farmer and His Almanac.** William Ware and Company, Boston, 1904.

Old Farmer's 1949 Almanac. No. 157. Yankee, Inc., Dublin, New Hampshire, 1948.

Pickard, Madge E., and Buley, R. C., *The Midwest Pioneer: His Ills, Cures, Doctors.* R. E. Banta, Crawfordville, Indiana, 1945.

Pound, Louise, "Nebraska Rain Lore and Rain Making," *California Folklore Quarterly,* V (April, 1946), pp. 129-142.

_____, _____, "Nebraska Snake Lore," *Southern Folklore Quarterly,* X (Sept., 1946), pp. 163-176.

Reynold, Robert, *Grandma's Handbook,* (Tennessee Wesleyan College). Tennessee Folklore Society, Athens, Tennessee, March, 1950.

Thorndike, Lynn, *A History of Magic and Experimental Science,* 6 Vols. Macmillan, New York, 1923.

Zingara Fortune Teller: A Complete Treatise on the Art of Predicting Future Events, by A Gypsy Queen. David McKay, Philadelphia, 1901.

Suggestions for Further Study and for Collecting

1. What are oft-heard folk rules for acquiring wealth, preserving health, sharpening the wits, developing a strong character, picking a good mate, and rearing children?

2. How can one unravel his future through the meanings of his dreams?

3. What are folk cures for hiccups, for colds, for a sore throat, for indigestion, for bee sting, for snake bite, for rheumatism?

4. How, according to folklore, can one predict the sex of an unborn child, the identity of one's future husband or wife, and the location of buried treasure?

5. What weather signs are there to indicate the coming of storms, of clear weather, of hard winters, of hot summers, etc.?

6. What have been common methods followed by those witching for water, those who set up as rain-makers, and those who look for oil?

7. Study the lore connected with some trade or craft, such as the printer's, the jeweler's, or the truck driver's.

8. What is the technique of palmistry, of phrenology, of tea-leaf reading?

9. How has astrology been developed and how extensively is it used today?

10. What rules are there for planting and harvesting grains, melons, potatoes, or other crops?

CHAPTER TEN

CUSTOMS, RITUALS, AND CEREMONIES

Definitions and Comments

Whether in primitive societies or in the most sophisticated, the everyday lives of people in their personal relationships are controlled more by custom than by law or by reason. The crises of life—birth, marriage, death, etc.—are surrounded with ritualistic or ceremonial practices designed originally to make them more memorable, easier for associates, or less subject to evil influences. Social contacts are made less irritating and more delightful by "good manners" taught to children or learned by imitation as life goes on. Proper introductions, greetings, and leave-takings follow folk patterns.

We think of our code of daily behavior as etiquette, matters of courtesy; but much of it is ritual, determined historically through folklore. The folk behavior of different nations can be illustrated by the variation between European and American handling of eating implements, the difference between English and American greetings over the telephone.

All religions have their rituals and ceremonies. The learned tradition today includes a record of most of them, especially for those that are ancient and firmly established. But variations in actual practice are noticeable in connection with revivals, testimonial meetings, and baptisms as carried on by some of the more independent groups in remote districts. The Holy Week observances of the Penitentes in New Mexico and southern Colorado, for example, follow folk tradition rather than established church discipline.

Ritualistic dancing is still practiced by American Indians; although the war dance is used no more, except for display, the rain dance, the corn dance, etc., are performed at appropriate times in the pueblos of the Southwest. Initiation ceremonies for young people arriving at puberty have largely been replaced by school "commencements." In the United States' upper economic circles, the folk rituals of female initiation—the "coming-out party"—and of marriage are elaborate and expensive. Coming-out parties are less common than formerly, but a "shower" for the bride-to-be and a "stag party" for the prospective groom are still common. House-warmings are often held, and an occasional couple has to endure a charivari.

The extra buttons and loops of our ordinary clothing have their reasons in folklore rather than in aesthetics or utility. Rules for the proper dress on different occasions—"black tie with dinner coat"—and for ways of wearing clothing—"the bottom button of the vest must be unbuttoned"—are matters of folk ritual. Courtly circles once followed an elaborate code, that of the Middle Ages being called chivalry. The folk has usually been less formal but none the less respectful toward the established ways of group intercourse.

67

Basic Readings* and General References
Allsop, Fred, *Folklore of Romantic Arkansas.* Grolier Society, Chicago, 1931.
Breakenridge, William A., *Helldorado, Bringing the Law to the Mesquite.* Houghton Mifflin, Boston, 1928.
Brendaur, Effie, *Death Customs.* Knopf, New York, 1930.
Eichler, Lillian, *The Customs of Mankind.** Doubleday, Doran, Garden City, New York, 1924.
Hand, Wayland D., "Folklore, Customs and Traditions of the Butte Miner." *California Folklore Quarterly,* V (Jan., 1946), pp. 1-26 and (April, 1946), pp. 153-178.
Hastings, John, editor, *Encyclopedia of Religion and Ethics.* Scribners, New York, 1924-27.
Kane, Harnett T., *Deep Delta Country.* Duell, Sloan and Pearce, New York, 1944.
(cf. others in this popular *American Folkways Series.)*
Leyburn, James G., *Frontier Folkways.* Yale University Press, New Haven, Conn., 1935.
Nebraska Folklore Pamphlets, No. 26, *Pioneer Religion.* Historical Society, Lincoln, Nebraska, 1940.
Post, Emily, *Etiquette.** Funk and Wagnalls, New York, 1922 and later.
Pound, Louise, "Old Nebraska Folk Customs." *Nebraska History,* XXVIII, (Jan.-March, 1947), pp. 3-31.
Sapir, Edward, *Selected Writings in Language, Culture and Personality,* edited by David G. Mandelbaum. University of California Press, Berkeley, 1949.
Saxon, Lyle, *Old Louisiana.* Appleton, Century, New York, 1929.
Shippey, Lee, *It's an Old California Custom.* The Vanguard Press, New York, 1948. (cf. others in this popular *American Customs Series.)*

Sumner, William Graham, *Folkways.** Ginn, Boston, 1906.

Titiev, M., "Two Hopi Myths and Rites," *Journal of American Folklore,* LXI (Jan.-March, 1948), pp. 19-30.

Voiles, James, "Genoese Folkways in a California Mining Camp," *California Folklore Quarterly,* III (July, 1944), pp. 212-216.

Walsh, William S., *Curiosities of Popular Customs and Rites, Ceremonies, Observances and Miscellaneous Antiquities.* Lippincott, Philadelphia, 1898.

Westermarck, E., *The History of Human Marriage.* Macmillan, London, 5th ed., 1921.

Suggestions for Further Study and for Collecting

1. Discuss the origin of some familiar customs—such as shaking hands, bowing, tipping the hat, walking on the "outside" with a lady.

2. Examine several editions of Emily Post's *Etiquette* and show how customs have changed. For example, what effect did World War II have on custom?

3. Describe the customs, rituals, and ceremonies considered proper at funerals, birthday parties, or picnics?

4. How did the customs of some primitive society differ from those of some modern sophisticated culture?

5. What are the customs surrounding some of the life crises: birth, marriage, death, etc.?

6. Show how some of these customs at life crises vary among different cultural or racial groups.

7. What special customs are traditionally practiced in your home? What is their origin? e.g. preparation for going to bed, arranging for a dinner party, entertaining callers, giving gifts on certain occasions.

8. Do you know of any customs which are peculiarly American—perhaps growing out of certain stages in American history? e.g. barbecues, camp meetings, the trappers' rendezvous.

9. What elements are common in the rituals and ceremonies of special groups such as fraternities and lodges?

10. What is a scapegoat? bundling? potlatch?

11. How does custom regulate the behavior of children at play, boy-girl relationships in schools, or courtships in various parts of our country?

12. What ceremonies exist for blessing the fields or a fishing expedition?
13. What ceremonies are conducted at the dedication of a building or monument, at the laying of a cornerstone, at the graduation of a senior class?
14. Do groups of boys, girls, tramps, or outlaws have any customary tests for memberships?
15. What ceremonies of purification, of fasting, of prayer are common to a number of religions that you know about?
16. Why is it customary to throw rice at newly-weds, for the bride to wear a veil, to give blue ribbons to boy babies, and to wear black for mourning?
17. What would be violations of good manners at a dance, at meals, while spending a week-end at a friend's home?

CHAPTER ELEVEN

FOLK DRAMAS, FESTIVALS, AND HOLIDAYS

Definitions and Comments

Actual folk drama has had but a meagre part in the popular entertainments of American communities. Spanish colonists did bring over from Europe some traditional religious plays, such as those given at Easter and at Christmas to illustrate the biblical stories; the descendants of the Spanish later developed a few folk dramas on secular themes, such as Indian raids. The Spanish influence extended through New Mexico and up into the San Luis valley of Colorado. Penitente enactment of the crucifixion is still a dramatic folk event in many communities of the Southwest. So-called "folk drama" today is written and staged by individual artists and by trained actors using folk life and folk ways to portray, somewhat realistically, regional differences.

Some American communities have imported and translated "Passion Plays" from Germany and elsewhere and perform them annually, as semi-professional community projects. In addition, many local pageants containing dramatic dialogue, incidental music, costuming, and dances, and sometimes written as well as performed by amateurs, manifest our growing interest in our own history and folk traditions. Outstanding is the annual performance of *The Lost Colony,* a drama about the

Roanoke settlement written by Paul Green. These dramas, like the flamboyant staging in Deadwood, S. D., of the "Trial of Jack McCall," are intended to draw tourists for the commercial betterment of the "home folk," a purpose not entirely absent from present-day European or American Passion Plays.

Among the popular entertainments of a dramatic nature that have had a long life in the United States are the patent-medicine show, the Negro minstrel show, and the "Punch and Judy" or marionette show. Rodeos, parades, lodge initiations, country fairs, band concerts, street carnivals, exhibitions of magic, and circuses have had dramatic appeal and have developed traditional features.

Festivals, also, are common occurrences. Nearly every community still has its harvest festival or local feast day— "Melon Day," "Homecoming," "Old-timers Reunion," "Mardi Gras," "Frontier Days," "De Vargas Day," or "Founders' Day." Pageantry, if not pageants, is a common feature of these festivals, with the folk costuming themselves in the styles of their ancestors, or in fantastic and gaudy apparel, even organizing ritualistic societies for the celebration of Mardi Gras in New Orleans and Mummers' Day in Philadelphia. Imposed folk customs, like the growing of beards and the wearing of western or "Gay '90's" costumes, for a town's or university's "Founders' Day," are observed on some of these occasions.

The holidays—seasonal and church—observed in European countries are for the most part continued in the new world; these include Christmas, Easter, All Fools' Day, and Valentine's Day. Then, too, new ones of a patriotic nature have been established, such as the Fourth of July, Washington's Birthday, Armistice Day, and

73

Memorial Day. Labor Day, Arbor Day, and Poppy Day are only a few of those with a special function; some activities require a longer time, e.g. "Clean-up Week."

A number of the American folk holidays of the past century, some of which are still observed, incorporated typically European features, like the Italian parades with religious banners and brass bands on Columbus Day, the parading and arraying of the Irish in green on St. Patrick's Day, the German *schutzenfesten* (shooting-contests) and family picnics on mid-summer holidays. But American celebrations have had a distinctive mixture of "spread-eagle" oratory, patriotic parades, fireworks in the evening, band concerts, and sometimes, such sports as baseball games between "Married Men" and "Bachelors."

Folk entertainments and festivals also include school exhibition programs, box suppers, Legion conventions, community picnics, and other activities devised by the people, of the people, and for the people. The methods followed become traditional with the group concerned.

Basic Readings* and General References

Campa, Arthur L., *Spanish Religious Folktheatre in the Spanish Southwest,* First and Second Cycles. University of New Mexico Bulletins, Albuquerque, 1934.

.............., ..., *Los Comanches: A New Mexican Folk Drama.* University of New Mexico Bulletins, Albuquerque, 1942.

Chambers, Robert, *The Book of Days.** 2 Vols., W. and R. Chambers, London and Edinburg, 1864-66.

Cole, M. R., *Los Pastores: A Mexican Play of the Nativity.* American Folklore Society, Boston, 1907.

Douglas, George W., *The American Book of Days.** H. W. Wilson Company, New York, 1940.

Folk Festival Handbook: A Practical Guide for Local Communities. The Evening Bulletin, Philadelphia, 1944.

Gilbert, Douglas, *American Vaudeville: Its Life and Times.* Whittlesey House, New York, 1940.

Hazeltine, Mary E., *Anniversaries and Holidays.** American Library Association, Chicago, 1944.

Koch, Frederick H., *Carolina Folk-Plays* (First-Third Series). Henry Holt, New York, 1941.

McCleery, Albert, and Glick, Carl, *Curtain's Going Up, "Theatre Americana."* Pitman, New York and Chicago, 1939.

McNeal, Violet, *Four White Horses and a Brass Band.* Doubleday, Garden City, New York, 1947.

McSpadden, J. W., *The Book of Holidays.* Crowell, New York, 1917.

Paskman, Dailey, and Spaeth, Sigmund, *Gentlemen, Be Seated.* Doubleday, Garden City, New York, 1928.

75

Spicer, Dorothy G., *The Book of Festivals*. The Woman's Press, New York, 1937.

Sper, Felix, *From Native Roots: A Panorama of Our Regional Drama*.* The Caxton Printers, Caldwell, Idaho, 1948.

Tallant, Robert, *Mardi Gras*. Doubleday, Garden City, New York, 1948.

Theatre Arts, August, 1950, "Regional Theatre 1950," pp. 25-91.

Wittke, Carl F., *Tambo and Bones: A History of the American Minstrel Stage*. Duke University Press, Durham, North Carolina, 1930.

Suggestions for Further Study and for Collecting

1. What are the customary ways of celebrating Christmas, Easter, New Year's Day, April First, Memorial Day, Thanksgiving Day, or July 4th?

2. What are the common elements in patriotic parades? bathing beauty contests? political campaigns? lodge and fraternity initiations?

3. What are the popular dramatic elements in sports spectacles such as the World's Series in baseball, or a football game between Army and Navy, or a heavyweight prize fight, or the Olympics?

4. Where is the Passion Play still performed? How does it resemble the folk dramas of the Middle Ages?

5. Describe the festivals held each year in your community. Contrast them to the special events of some other region.

6. What is the National Folk Festival, directed by Sarah Gertrude Knott, and what is its history?

7. Discuss the folk gatherings of our pioneer forefathers. How did they lighten labor and amuse themselves at barn-raisings, round-ups, quilting parties, sugaring-off parties, hunting parties, etc.?

8. Do you know of any groups of workers that celebrate holidays as groups or that have developed programs for their own entertainment?

9. What types of dramatic activities are common in home-talent shows? In church festivals for raising money? In campaigns for community charities?

10. What saints are remembered by special days, and how are these days observed? e.g. Saint Patrick's Day.

77

CHAPTER TWELVE

FOLK MUSIC, DANCES, AND GAMES

Definitions and Comments

When the folk entertain themselves they dance, play games, and make music. Singing may be a part of these entertainments; but, since songs and ballads are considered elsewhere, instrumental music is emphasized here. Children, especially, play games both indoor and out, with or without singing and rhyming accompaniments. When people get older they engage in sports. In folk cultures they participate in tests of strength, agility, and cunning; in advanced societies they spend much time watching or reading about the competition of professional athletes. Gambling upon the outcome of games is universal.

The origin of many games, like that of drama and the dance, is attributed to religious and magical practices, a ritual propitiation and honoring of gods, heroes, and natural forces. Although now forgotten, these religious features of games may still be detected by anthropological analysis. Another theory of the origin of games is that they were used to train the young and drill the braves of the tribe in sport and war. We find elements of both origins in playing cards. Their symbols are suspected of being magical, as can be seen in their use in fortune telling. Card suits symbolized armies and were used to teach military strategy, as were chess and checkers. Goalgames, also, like football and hockey, were originally associated with a struggle for a sacred object in festivals and were used later as training for war. Archery, now a sport, was once a preparation of the English folk for national defense. Many of our modern, organized, commercialized sports show a long history of folk development from pre-historic times; basketball, for example, is similar to the more complicated Aztec court games.

Dramatic and ritualistic elements survive in children's games and in sports organized for special occasions, like the Greek and modern Olympics. Many American occupational sports have practical significance; these include work "bees" connected with harvests (husking bees), and with house-raisings, the rodeo, the miners' and loggers' displays of their skills at tournaments, and the out-moded hose-cart races by volunteer firemen.

Hand-made musical instruments, like the old-time fiddles, banjos, zithers, and guitars, have largely been replaced in the United States by factory produced ones and by pianos, violins, accordions, and mouth-organs. They yield up folk music, however, when played by non-professional folk musicians, those who just picked up their skills and their tunes without schooling, usually by ear rather than from printed notes. Fiddle tunes, show pieces, and song melodies have all been subject to collection and study by folklorists.

Distinctive American additions to folk music are the Negroes' combination of African and European rhythms into jazz at the end of the 19th century and the "shape note" notation of hymns for the Southern Mountain singing schools. Although smoothed out and commercialized by popular dance bands, jazz has continually drawn strength from the unwritten improvisations of "natural," though paid, folk musicians. Because it is close to antiphonal and polyphonal medieval and ultra-modern music, European intellectuals have acclaimed jazz as livelier and greater than our country's less original, conventional melodic compositions. In other areas of American folk music, tunes have been transmitted by ear, virtually without change, as in the cases of "Old Dan Tucker" and "The Arkansas Traveller." Today, we can expect to find the music as well as the words of folk ballads "arranged" for commercial presentation. "Tin Pan Alley" has drawn on folk music more or less success-fully, and continually, since Stephen Foster.

Although ritualistic dancing for religious purposes and imitative dancing for power in the hunt have largely disappeared in the United States, social dancing is an important part of folk life today. Folk dances are also very popular among square dance groups and at sophis-ticated parties. Old-time dances and those imported by more recent immigrants are demonstrated at the annual National Folk Festival and elsewhere to the delight of participants and audiences.

A once-popular substitute for social dancing was the play party. It avoided the use of fiddle music, regarded as of the devil, and close contact between male and female dancers. Various evolutions were performed to the rhythm of a song of chanted words, something like children's singing games.

Basic Readings* and General References

Bayard, Samuel P., *Hill Country Tunes.* Memoir 39, American Folklore Society, Philadelphia, 1944.

Botkin, Ben A., *The American Play-Party Song.* University of Nebraska, Lincoln, Nebraska, 1937.

Buchanan, Annabel Morris, *American Folk Music.* National Federation of Music Clubs, Ithaca, New York, 1939.

Burchenal, Elizabeth, *American Country Dances.* G. Schirmer, New York, 1918.

Chase, Richard, *Old Songs and Singing Games.* University of North Carolina, Chapel Hill, North Carolina, 1938.

Czarnowski, Lucile K., *Dances of Early California Days.* Pacific Books, Palo Alto, California, 1950.

Folk Music of the United States and Latin America. Catalog of Phonographic Records in Library of Congress, Washington, D. C., 1948.

Ford, Ira W., *Traditional Music of America.* E. P. Dutton, New York, 1940.

Ferguson, Erna, *Dancing Gods.* Knopf, New York, 1931.

Herzog, George, *Research in Primitive and Folk Music in the U. S.* Bulletin 24, American Council of Learned Societies, Washington, D. C., 1936.

Duggan, Anne Schley, Schlottmann, Jeanette, and Rutledge, Abbie, *The Folk Dance Library,* 5 V. A. S. Barnes, New York, 1948.

Howard, John Tasher, *Our American Music.* T. Y. Crowell, New York, 1931.

Hunt, Sarah, and Cain, Ethel, *Games the World Around.* A. S. Barnes, New York, 1941.

Kittle, J. Leslie, "Authentic Form of Folk Music in

Colorado." *Colorado Magazine*, Denver, V. XXII, 1945, pp. 59-63.

Lovett, Mr. and Mrs. Benjamin B., *Good Morning: Music, Calls, and Directions for Old-Time Dancing.* Henry Ford, Dearborn, Michigan, 1926.

Maloney, Violetta G., "Jumping Rope Rhymes from Burley, Idaho." *Hoosier Folklore*, V.iii, 1944, pp. 24-25.

Mason, Bernard S., and Mitchell, Elmer D., *Social Games for Recreation.* A. S. Barnes, New York, 1935.

Mayo, Margot, *The American Square Dance.* Sentinel Books, New York, 1948.

McIntosh, David S., *Southern Illinois Songs and Games.* Southern Illinois Normal University, Carbondale, Illinois, 1946.

Owens, William A., *Swing and Turn: Texas Play-Party Games.* Tardy Publishing Co., Dallas, Texas, 1936.

Ramsey, Frederic, and Smith, Charles E., *Jazzmen.* Harcourt, Brace, New York, 1939.

Shaw, Lloyd, *Cowboy Dances.** Caxton Printers, Caldwell, Idaho, 1939.

Withers, Carl, *A Rocket in My Pocket: The Rhymes and Chants of Young Americans.* Henry Holt, New York, 1948.

Wood, Clement, *The Complete Book of Games.** Halcyon House, Garden City, New York, 1940.

Wood, Ray, *The American Mother Goose.* Frederick A. Stokes, New York, 1940.

Suggestions for Further Study and for Collecting

1. Describe the national dances of various countries.
2. Collect the children's games of your childhood and compare them with those of today. How many remain unchanged? What new games have been added?
3. Make a collection of adult party games played by your friends. Where did they learn the games?
4. Try to trace the history of various popular folk dances and their different forms.
5. What are some of the more famous square-dance groups in the United States? What is their history— i.e., how did they get started, etc.?
6. Find out all you can about some of the famous performers of folk-song and music of modern times: Richard Dyer-Bennett, Burl Ives, John Jacob Niles, Lead Belly, Josh White, Carl Sandburg, Alan Lomax, Pete Seeger, and Woody Guthrie.
7. Collect some of the more colorful calls used by square-dance callers.
8. Discuss the use made of folk music by professional composers in orchestral pieces, in the opera *(Porgy and Bess),* and in musical comedies *(Oklahoma).*
9. Discuss the use made of folk themes by professional choreographers—for example, in the ballet *Frankie and Johnny, Billy the Kid,* or *Rodeo.*
10. Look into the history of such games as chess, football, basketball, and baseball. What is thought to have been their original forms and purposes?
11. What is the history of such American forms of music as the blues, jazz, and boogie-woogie?
12. How does one play charades, anagrams, treasure hunt, marbles, forfeits, and jackstones?

CHAPTER THIRTEEN

ARTS AND CRAFTS

Definitions and Comments

In primitive societies and in frontier communities the folk devised for themselves, usually in traditional patterns, whatever they needed in the way of tools, housing, clothing, adornments, and food. Their handicrafts and their folk arts, which grew out of the desire to add beauty to utility, have been largely replaced by factory production and by designs created by individuals trained in schools of fine arts or in trade schools. Much of value, however, resides in the old designs and in the old techniques. As with the verbal folklore previously studied, these non-verbal folk arts and skills provide resources for rich human living and for sophisticated art forms. Indeed, the folk crafts, by providing skills and hobbies for the white-collar worker, the physically handicapped and those mentally "in a rut," are still important means to culture and to psychic health for great numbers of people who do not think of themselves as either scholars of the folk tradition or as artists.

Many people today are interested in antiques, in the hand products of American Indians, in the hand-woven fabrics of the southern mountaineers, and in the survival of earlier American furniture patterns, architectural features, architectural hardware, and house types. Old-time musical instruments, devised and made by the folk, are collected and even played on.

American Indian handicrafts, characterized by decorative elaborations on weapons, tools and other useful objects, and by the use of symbols expressive of the Indians' religious identification with non-human parts of nature, are well represented among the art objects in the world's museums. Indian craftsmanship varied from tribe to tribe—or rather, from culture to culture—with the more settled and less nomadic Indian cultures presenting more artistically meaningful handicrafts. Indian crafts like pottery and weaving, still carried on in the Southwest, are of ancient date and in their older and less commercial practice contained designs of folk origins. Making of jewelry with hand tools was specially developed by the Indians of Mexico and the United States after the Spaniards had acquainted the southwestern tribes with coin silver. The Indians' sand paintings were magical, intended to cure ills; it was part of the working of their magic that they be erased as soon as they were made, the decorative aspect being a "side issue."

Included under traditional feminine skills—called housewifery—are cookery, costume or dress making, weaving, house furnishing, securing such equipment as silverware and dishes for the table, and the making of decorative objects such as samplers, pictures, drapery, and jewelry. There is an interesting history covering each of these classes of objects before they were taken over by factory and mass production.

In cookery, the United States today is an inheritor of the folk craft of the world. Whether the housewife prepares her meals from raw materials or out of cans, she has a wide selection of European and Oriental dishes. Our menus today contain a mingling of the favorite dishes of all sections of our nation—New England, Pennsylvania, the South, etc. These recipes were developed out of the peculiar resources of each region or borrowed from Indian cookery and the folk cuisine of the dominant European settlers of each region.

American drinks are a folk craft in themselves. Whether alcoholic or non-alcoholic, they, like other kinds of folklore, contain a mixture of borrowings from Europe and purely native elements. Herb teas and "swizzle" (vinegar and molasses-flavored water drunk by harvesters) show adaptations of European folk wisdom to our climate. Bourbon (corn) whiskey was made and drunk on the American frontier. The mixture called a "cocktail" is, for better or worse, world-renowned as an American invention. Even more American are the imaginative concoctions of our soda fountains, whose history and "mixology" have not yet been formally studied. Coca-cola and American cigarettes are products of our industrial-commercial culture; their use is a modern "folkway" that has spread far beyond our borders.

Under husbandry, in the masculine province, come agricultural traditions, the securing and use of outdoor tools, weapons of all kinds, the domestication of animals, and the development of various trades and occupations for earning a living.

Food and drink, costumes and decorations, dwellings and other enclosures have their artistic as well as their functional aspects. The forms, colors, textures, designs, and materials that are used in baskets, rugs, or jewelry have often been established by custom; they may have traditional symbolic meanings. Such objects are used in rituals and ceremonies as well as in daily life.

Different regions have their own special arts and crafts, depending upon natural resources, climate, original sources of population groups, economic and social conditions, and level of development. Modern standardization is destroying some of these differences; others are tenaciously cherished.

Basic Readings* and General References

Atwater, Mary Meigs, *The Shuttle-craft Book of American Hand-weaving.* Macmillan, New York, 1928.

Bowles, Mrs. E. S., *Homespun Handicrafts.* J. B. Lippincott, Philadelphia, 1931.

Burdette, Kay, *Cookery of the Old South.* Baytown, Texas, 1941.

Coffin, R. P. T., *Mainstays of Maine.* Macmillan, New York, 1944.

Cooper, Virginia M., *Creole Kitchen Cook Book.* San Antonio, Texas, 1941.

Dickey, Roland F., *New Mexico Village Arts.* University of New Mexico, Albuquerque, 1949.

Douglas, Frederic H., *Indian Leaflet Series,* "Indian Sand-Painting," etc. Denver Art Museum, Denver, reprinted, 1947.

Drepperd, C. W., *American Pioneer Arts and Artists.* Pond-Ekberg, Springfield, Mass., 1932.

Eaton, Allen H., *Immigrant Gifts to American Life.* William F. Fell, New York, 1932.

------------, ----------------, *Handicrafts of the Southern Highlands.* Russell Sage Foundation, New York, 1937.

--------------------------, *Handicrafts of New England.* Harper Bros., New York, 1949.

Eberlein, Harold D., and McClure, Abbot, *The Practical Book of American Antiques.* Lippincott, Philadelphia, 1947.

Evans, Mary, *Costume Throughout the Ages.* Lippincott, Philadelphia, 1938.

Haire, Frances, and Moser, Gertrude, *The Folk Costume Book.** A. S. Barnes, New York, 1926.

Hunt, Walter B., *Indian and Camp Handicraft*. Bruce Publishing Co., New York, 1938.

Lipman, Jean, *American Folk Art*.* Pantheon, New York, 1948.

Mackey, Margaret G., and Sooy, Louise P., *Early California Costumes (1769-1847)*. Stanford University Press, Stanford, California, 1932.

Morphy, Marcelle, *Recipes of All Nations*.* William H. Wise, New York, 1935.

Nebraska Folklore Pamphlet, No. 28, *Folk Cooking*. W. P. A. project, State Historical Society, Lincoln, 1940.

New Bartender's Guide. I. and M. Ottenheimer, Baltimore, 1914.

Pennsylvania Dutch Cook Book. Culinary Arts Press, Reading, Pennsylvania, 1936.

Robinson, Ethel F., *Houses in America*. Viking, New York, 1936.

Robertson, Elizabeth Wells, *American Quilts*. The Studio Publications, New York, 1948.

Rollins, Philip A., *The Cowboy: His Equipment and His Part in the Development of the West*. Scribners, New York, 1936.

Toor, Frances, *Mexican Popular Arts*. Frances Toor Studios, Mexico, D. F., 1939.

Train, Arthur, Jr., *The Story of Everyday Things*.* Harper Bros., New York, 1941.

Underhill, Ruth, *Pueblo Crafts*. Phoenix Indian School, Phoenix, Arizona, 1945.

Williamson, Scott G., *The American Craftsman*. Crown, New York, 1940.

Suggestions for Further Study and for Collecting

1. What handicrafts are still carried on in your community? By women? By men? By children? What imported handicraft objects are on sale in city stores?
2. How much of the cooking done in your home is done according to cookbook and how much according to traditional ways? Where did the recipes come from?
3. Describe common tools, kitchen and table equipment, farm and shop instruments, showing basic folk patterns.
4. What parts of a cowboy's equipment are functional and what are for show? What of an Indian's clothing?
5. How have climate and the availability of certain materials influenced the dietary habits of people in different sections of the United States?
6. What differences in architectural styles are there between New England, the Deep South, the Southwest, California, and Alaska?
7. What crafts were practiced in colonial days that have disappeared since? Which were primarily utilitarian and which primarily ornamental or artistic?
8. Describe the different types of fences, hay-loaders, and barns that have been used in our country.
9. What handicrafts are taught in schools or hospitals today?
0. How can one tell genuine antiques or hand-made articles from manufactured ones? Furniture? Jewelry? Silver and gold ware? Indian blankets, baskets, and beadwork? Embroidered garments?

CHAPTER FOURTEEN

HOW AND WHAT TO COLLECT

Comments and Suggestions

One does not need to depend upon books for knowledge of folklore. Even in the most sophisticated circles one can find it; and, without traveling very far, one can collect traditional materials that duplicate those published in standard works and can find local variations of great interest. By becoming a collector the student learns how folklore fits into the life of individuals and groups. His contacts with all sorts of folks should be entertaining and enlightening to him; his recordings may add to the store of available folklore for others to study and to enjoy.

One should choose a topic or a type of folklore for study and, after reading what is available on the subject, begin the collection of examples. The general relationship of the chosen segment of the field to folklore as a whole should, however, be kept in mind. The purpose may be to collect all the versions one can find of a particular folk song, tale, remedy, or other piece of specific lore; or one may desire to collect all of the different kinds of traditional lore to be found in a given locality, such as a town or county; or one may wish to study the culture imported from a foreign country, e.g., Italian customs and festivals in some American city. By reading all available collections and discussions of the type of lore the student plans to collect, he is better prepared to draw out an informant and to sort out the valuable from the irrelevant.

Oral sources may be tapped in informal conversations or by specially arranged interviews. The former method reveals much of folk speech, beliefs, and customs; the latter leads to songs and ballads, myths and legends, tales, and music. By observation one learns about arts and crafts, festivals, holiday observances, rituals and ceremonies. Correspondence may be used to supplement oral conferences, to open up leads, and to follow up subjects incompletely covered. Much folklore can be gleaned from old manuscripts, diaries, autobiographies, newspapers and other publications, both current and from earlier periods. But it is folklore only if it has once been a part of the popular folk heritage.

Beginning with one's family and friends, the collector gradually extends his contacts. He should always record carefully the nature of his sources, the ages and backgrounds of the people interviewed, the time and place, the questions used, the exact answers. Material should be taken down as rapidly as possible, it should be written up in full as soon after the interview as possible, and no attempt should be made to improve upon it or to polish it. A friendly, informal manner will produce better results than will a learned, formal, or superior attitude. Various types and makes of sound recording machines are on the market—disc, tape, wire—and they are quite useful and accurate, especially in recording music and speech sounds. The Folklore Section of the Library of Congress has had much experience with recordings and should be consulted by those interested. Photographs, also, are valuable supplements to verbal descriptions of customs and folk arts.

As one becomes known as a collector, he will receive many suggestions of possible informants to interview. Local newspapers and radio stations may be willing to cooperate by circulating examples of the type of folklore desired and then requesting that additional versions and similar folklore be sent to the collector. Teachers and pupils in the public schools of Arizona, for example, have helped folklorists at the University of Arizona to assemble many kinds of material from the oral traditions of their state.

In preparation for the future use of collected materials, classification and systematic filing are necessary. Each item should be properly identified and labeled. Some collectors use three copies, putting one under the name of the informant in an alphabetical classification of sources, one under the proper heading by types, and one in a file arranged by ethnic groups or by localities. As subdivisions one could use the "Index of Tale Types" and "Index of Motifs" in Stith Thompson's *The Folktale;* the song titles or numbers in Child's *English and Scottish Popular Ballads* and some American collections such as Belden's *Ballads and Songs Collected by the Missouri Folk-Lore Society* or John and Alan Lomax' *Folk Song: U. S. A.;* and the classifications in Sean O'Suilleabhain's *A Handbook of Irish Folklore.* Each collector will devise his own system for filing manuscript materials, clippings, pamphlets, and books. A poor system or a careless use of even a good one will lead to much waste of time.

Collected material is valueless to others unless the folklore collector puts it into circulation. It can be organized into newspaper reports, radio programs, magazine articles, talks for general audiences or for folklore societies, scholarly articles for folklore journals and books. It can then be studied in class rooms and by individuals. Out of the contributions of many collectors and of many scholars there will finally emerge a greater knowledge of American folklore and a greater appreciation of it.

Basic Readings* and General References

American Dialect Society, *Needed Research in American English*. Address Secretary, Greensboro, North Carolina, 1943.

Bercovici, Konrad, *Around the World in New York.** Century, New York, 1924.

Blegen, T. C., and Rund, M. B., *Norwegian Emigrant Songs and Ballads*. University of Minnesota Press, Minneapolis, Minnesota, 1936.

Botkin, Ben A., "Living Lore on the New York City Writer's Project," *New York Folklore Quarterly,* II (Nov., 1946), pp. 252-263.

Brewster, Paul G., *Ballads and Songs of Indiana*. Indiana University Publications, Bloomington, Indiana, 1940.

Bryant, Margaret M., *Proverbs and How to Collect Them.** Publications of the American Dialect Society, IV (Nov., 1945), Greensboro, North Carolina.

Davis, A. K., *Traditional Ballads of Virginia: Collected under the Auspices of the Virginia Folklore Society*. Harvard University Press, Cambridge, Mass., 1929.

Gardner, Evelyn E., *Folklore from the Schoharie Hills*. University of Michigan Press, Ann Arbor, Michigan, 1937.

Hoogasian, Susie, and Gardner, Evelyn E., "Armenian Folktales from Detroit," *Journal of American Folklore,* 57 (July-Sept., 1944), pp. 161-180.

Ives, Burl, *Wayfaring Stranger: An Autobiography*. Whittlesey House, New York, 1948.

Lichten, Frances, *Folk Art of Rural Pennsylvania*. Scribners, New York, 1946.

Lomax, John, *Adventures of a Ballad Hunter.** Macmillan, New York, 1947.

97

Mackenzie, W. Roy, *The Quest of the Ballad.* Princeton University Press, Princeton, N. J., 1919.

O'Suilleabhain, Sean, *A Handbook of Irish Folklore.** Irish Folklore Commission, Dublin, 1942.

Preston, D. R., *Folklore of American Cities.* Howell-Soskin, New York, 1948.

Scarborough, Dorothy A., *A Song Catcher in Southern Mountains.* Columbia University Press, New York, 1937.

Sickels, Alice L., *Around the World in St. Paul.** University of Minnesota Press, Minneapolis, Minnesota, 1945.

Stout, Earl J., *Folklore from Iowa.* Memoir 29, American Folklore Society, New York, 1936.

Thomas, Jean, *Ballad Makin' in the Mountains of Kentucky.* Henry Holt, New York, 1939.

Tully, Marjorie, and Rael, Juan B., *An Annotated Bibliography of Spanish Folklore in New Mexico and Southern Colorado.* University of New Mexico Press, Albuquerque, New Mexico, 1950.

Whitfield, Irene T., *Louisiana French Folk Songs.* Louisiana State University Press, Baton Rouge, La., 1937.

Suggestions for Further Study and for Collecting

1. Make a list of all the games you played as a child. How many of them are still popular? What folk remedies, superstitions, place legends, etc., did you know as a child?

2. Interview your friends after you have worked out a questionnaire designed to aid them in recalling the folklore that is a part of their heritage. As you travel, interview people with backgrounds different from your own.

3. Study the methods of such collectors as John Lomax, Carl Sandburg, Vance Randolph, or Burl Ives; much is revealed in their autobiographical notes as to how they talked and listened—when, where, and how.

4. Read several of the descriptive leaflets accompanying folksong records put out by the Folklore Section of the Library of Congress or by the commercial record companies, in order to find out what kind of data is usable.

5. Check through the files of the folklore journals for articles reporting collecting experiences. How have the authors of these articles discovered sources, conducted their interviews or recordings, and annotated their findings?

6. In what fields of folklore study do you think more collecting is needed? How much could be done in your community? Where could you begin?

7. As you listen to the radio, read the daily newspaper, or go about your work, note all references to folk sayings, folk wisdom, folk heroes, familiar anecdotes, superstitions, etc. Then check with printed versions to see if you have local variations.

8. When you attend weddings, funerals, commencements, patriotic programs, etc., record all of the traditional elements and see if you can trace them to their folk origins.

9. Study the examples of folk arts and crafts in art museums and historical exhibits. What elements are pleasing and why. What do these objects reveal about the ways of life of their makers?

10. Develop a filing system, using folders or envelopes labeled with the headings developed in your folklore index. You might use as major divisions the titles of the chapters in this guide, with sub-titles and additions to cover systematically the materials that you find and the special problems that you are studying.

CHAPTER FIFTEEN

THE UTILIZATION OF FOLKLORE

Comments and Suggestions

Folklore study should result in an appreciation of the contributions made to our culture by common, everyday people. Greater tolerance, also, of the many differences between the racial, regional, and economic groups in our country should develop as one learns the backgrounds from which these differences have emerged. Provincialism is lessened by a knowledge of other ways of life. Folklore study is not merely an analysis of quaint survivals from the past, but a democratic method for using whatever of human interest may be found in the diverse cultures that exist in our land today.

The entertainment values in folklore are obvious. Nearly everyone enjoys folksongs, folktales, proverbs, humorous anecdotes, old-time games, folk dances, quaint but authentic works of folk artists and craftsmen, and bits of traditional wisdom. The folk song has been brought to the concert platform, the radio, the motion pictures, the night clubs, and the record companies in the United States by such well-known interpreters as John Jacob Niles, Richard Dyer-Bennet, Burl Ives, Josh White, Josef and Miranda Marais, Lead Belly, Pete Seeger, and many a less famous singer. At the national and regional folklore conferences and festivals both the audience and the performers have an enjoyable time, often exchanging places and mixing up in communal singing and dancing. But the old-time group or individual singing still functions in the lives of less sophisticated people, remote from the centers of commercialized entertainments. And the showing and admiring of handicrafts takes place daily in many less formal environments than museums and county fairs.

Creative artists have woven much folklore into their fiction, drama, or poetry; they have borrowed themes, colors, and designs for their paintings, architecture, or plastic arts; they have composed songs, orchestral pieces, musical dramas, and operas under the inspiration and the patterns of folk melodies, folk rhythms, folk instruments. In literature such masters as Hawthorne, Melville, Poe, and Mark Twain sent their roots down deep into native legend, folk beliefs, and popular speech. The paintings of Thomas Hart Benton, Grant Wood, George Biddle, and William Gropper are among those that have wide appeal largely because of their American folk subject matter. The folk inspiration of the songs and dances in such popular musical plays as *Oklahoma, Bloomer Girl,* and *Sing Out, Sweet Land* is obvious. Composers such as Anton Dvorak, Aaron Copland, Roy Harris, Virgil Thompson, and Henry Cowell have all used folk music as a basis for major works. And most historians treat "jazz" as a folk developed music. Motion pictures and dramas have recently included folk songs and folk characters. Not all utilization of folklore in modern art has been good, but the trend has been in the right direction.

Schools now use folklore in the teaching of history, international understanding, inter-cultural social relations, music, art, and literature. There are folk materials

102

and problems in folklore suitable for every level from the kindergarten to the graduate school. Teachers of the elementary and secondary levels weave folklore into the regular courses or projects rather than considering it as a separate subject.

Community centers, churches, and schools find that handicrafts, square dances, festivals, group singing, and "inter-national dinners," are popular social activities and prejudice dispellers. At the New York World's Fair thousands of visitors joined in simple folk dances on the American Common. During World War II, U. S. O. centers used folk dances as "mixers."

A knowledge of local folklore should enable one to put down roots and to draw strength from tradition. Familiarity with the folklore of other cultures should make one a citizen of the world. Folklore with its great diversity should, also, counteract to some degree the trend toward standardization characteristic of a machine age. Folklore study sometimes provides the key to an understanding both of popular fads and prejudices and of basic human desires and psychological needs.

*Basic Readings** and General References*

American Songs for American Children. Music Educators National Conference, 1942, 1944, 1946, etc.

Benét, Rosemary and Stephen, *A Book of Americans.* Rinehart, New York, 1933.

Baughman, Ernest W., "Folklore to the fore."* *The English Journal,* V. 32 (April, 1943), pp. 206-209.

Botkin, Ben A., "The Folk and the Individual: Their Creative Reciprocity." *The English Journal,* College Edition, XXVII (February, 1938), pp. 121-135.

Buchanan, Annabel Morris, "The Function of Folk Festivals." *Southern Folklore Quarterly,* V. 1 (March, 1937), pp. 29-34.

Cahill, Holger, *American Folk Art: The Art of the Common Man in America, 1750-1900.** Museum of Modern Art, New York, 1942.

Carmer, Carl, "American Folklore and Its Old-World Backgrounds" (together with Mary Gould Davis, "Following the Folk Tales Around the World"). Reprinted from *Compton's Pictured Encyclopedia,* Chicago, 1949.

——————, ——————, *America Sings: Stories and Songs of Our Country's Growing.* Knopf, New York, 1942.

Cox, John H., "Singing Games." *Southern Folklore Quarterly,* V. 6, December, 1942.

Curti, Merle, *The Growth of American Thought.* Harpers, New York, 1943.

Davidson, Levette J., "Folklore as a Supplement to Western History." *Nebraska History,* V. 29 (March, 1948) pp. 3-15.

Dubois, Rachel Davis, *Get Together Americans.* Harpers, New York, 1943.

_____, _____ _____, *Build Together Americans.* Hinds, Hayden, and Eldredge, New York, 1945.

Emrich, Marion V., and Korson, George, *The Child's Book of Folklore.** The Dial Press, New York, 1947.

Harrison, June, *Ancient Art and Ritual.* Oxford University Press, New York, 1913.

Jackson, George Pullen, and Bryan, Charles F., *American Folk Music for High School and Choral Groups.* C. C. Birchard and Company, Boston, 1947.

Jagendorf, M. A., *New England Bean-pot: American Folk Stories to Read and to Tell.* Vanguard, New York, 1948.

Jordan, Philip D., *Singin' Yankees.* University of Minnesota Press, Minneapolis, Minnesota, 1946.

Kluckhohn, Clyde, *Mirror for Man.* Whittlesey House, New York, 1949.

Miller, O. B., *Heroes, Outlaws, and Furry Fellows of American Popular Tales.* Doubleday, Garden City, New York, 1939.

Music Educators Journal. 6 times per year. 64 E. Jackson Blvd., Chicago.

Rourke, Constance, *American Humor.** Harcourt, Brace, New York, 1931.

_____, _____, *Roots of American Culture.* Harcourt, Brace, New York, 1942.

Saunders, Lyle, *A Guide to Materials Bearing on Cultural Relations in New Mexico.* University of New Mexico Press, Albuquerque, 1944.

Seeger, Ruth Crawford, *American Folk Songs for Children.* Doubleday, Garden City, New York, 1948.

Seldes, Gilbert, *The Seven Lively Arts.* Harpers, New York, 1924.

Shambaugh, Mary E., *Folk Festivals for Schools and Playground.* A. S. Barnes, New York, 1932.

Spaeth, Sigmund, *History of Popular Music.* Random House, New York, 1948.

*The Folk Festival Handbook: A Practical Guide for Local Communities.** Bulletin Co., Philadelphia, 1944.

Waugh, Coulton, *The Comics.* Macmillan, New York, 1947.

Wieard, Paul R., *Games of the Pennsylvania Germans.* Dept. of Public Playgrounds and Recreation, Reading, Pa.

Yoffie, Leah Rachel Clara, "Three Generations of Children's Singing Games in St. Louis." *Journal of American Folklore.* V. 60 (Jan.-March, 1947), pp. 1-51.

cf., Recordings of folk songs, folk music and musical compositions based upon folk materials, listed in the catalogs of Victor, Columbia, Disc, Decca, Asch, Keynote, and other recording companies.

cf., also, three folklore maps: William Gropper's "America, Its Folklore," Associated American Artists, 711 Fifth Ave., New York; Dorothea Dix Lawrence, "Folklore Music Map," Gramophone Shop, 183 48th St., New York; and M. E. Bush's *America Celebrates: A Travel Map of Festivals, Pageants and Special Events Best Reached by Greyhound.* Greyhound Lines, New York City and bus terminals in other cities, 1949.

Suggestions for Further Study and for Utilization

1. Analyze the methods used by Washington Irving in turning a folk legend into a short story—e.g. in "Rip Van Winkle," "The Devil and Tom Walker," and "The Legend of Sleepy Hollow"; by Hawthorne in "The Great Stone Face"; and by Mark Twain, "The Jumping Frog of Calaveras County."

2. Find modern short stories in books or magazines that reflect folk ways. Do they seem authentic?

3. Mark on a map of the United States the area supposedly roamed by each of our folk heroes. Different members of your group could then tell representative stories about these heroes.

4. Plan a vacation trip that will permit you to study the folklore of a traditional culture or a local festival.

5. What contributions to music have been made by the American Negro? What works by modern American composers use folk songs or melodies?

6. How did the streets in your home town or city get their names? Do they recall interesting history? What was the origin of the place-names on the map of your state?

7. What Spanish and Mexican dances have become popular in the United States?

8. Describe popular foods and methods for their preparation that have been introduced by immigrant groups to America. If native cooks are available ask them to demonstrate their traditional skills.

9. What cultures have used one of the following as a dietary base: corn, wheat, rice, potatoes, cabbage, fish, beef, lamb, buffalo, whale? In how many ways has each food been prepared?

10. Plan an old-fashioned colonial or frontier party, with folk dances, traditional games, folk customs, and traditional refreshments. Using folk patterns, sketch the costumes for a fancy dress ball, with different costumes representing different folk groups from the chief regions of the United States.
11. Put a local legend or tale into ballad form and set it to a traditional tune.
12. Design a wallpaper pattern by borrowing from the folk art of some American Indian tribe or of the Pennsylvania Dutch.
13. Learn the art of foretelling the future by palmistry, cards, dreams, or astrology. Then practice on your friends.
14. Start building a file of folklore materials, carefully indexed, with sources noted. It might be given to your local library later on.

FOLKLORE SCHOLARSHIP IN AMERICA

Folklore studies cover a wide range of subjects and involve the use of many different techniques and tools. Rather than attempting to formulate a limiting definition of what a scholar should or should not investigate, those interested in forwarding the extension of knowledge concerning folklore should analyze what has been done that has proved of lasting value. The references listed at the end of each chapter of this guide cover the outstanding examples. The careers of such great American folklorists as Francis J. Child, George Lyman Kittredge, Phillips Barry, Franz Boas, Archer Taylor, and Stith Thompson may be studied with profit. The files of the various folklore journals provide illustrations of nearly every possible field and method of research. And yet new topics and new approaches are developed every year.

Much good work has been accomplished in connection with folklore societies in America. Since the founding in 1888 of the American Folklore Society, numerous local or regional organizations have sprung up. Some have published magazines, such as the *Southern Folklore Quarterly*, organ of the Southeastern Folklore Society, or annual volumes, such as the annual *Publications of the Texas Folklore Society*. Nearly all have held annual meetings at which papers are read and folk music performed. Some have developed as sections of regional historical societies. The "Popular Literature" section of the Modern Language Association has emphasized folksong, folktale, and proverb research. The American Dialect Society has sponsored many group studies and has held annual meetings of interest to scholars of folk speech. The new series *Publications of the American Dialect Society* (No. 1, 1944—No. 13, 1950) has contained such articles as "Word-Lists from the South," "The Place-Names of Dane County, Wisconsin," "Oil Refinery Terms in Oklahoma," and "An Iowa Low German Dialect."

A few centers for folklore research have developed in America, especially in universities. At Indiana University, for example, a folklore curriculum leading to the master's and the doctor's degree was established in 1948, although many students had previously used folklore as a minor toward graduate degrees in English, linguistics, or anthropology. The Folklore Institute of America, also, has been held at Indiana University in the summers of 1942, 1946, and 1950, with visiting members on the faculty from various parts of America and from abroad. The "Seminars on American Culture" sponsored by the New York State Historical Association in Cooperstown during July in 1948, 1949, and 1950, included sections on "American Folklore," "American Folk Art," "Folklore Collecting," etc. "The Western Folklore Conference," held annually since 1941 at the University of Denver in connection with the Summer Session, features both the scholarly and the entertaining aspects of American folklore. The catalogs of such universities as North Carolina, California, Florida, Northwestern, Harvard, Columbia, Cornell, Wayne, Vanderbilt, Texas, Ohio State, Stanford, and New

Mexico contain announcements of courses in the departments of English, modern languages, history and anthropology that cover parts or all of the field of American folklore; but folklore departments or courses as such are comparatively rare.

Cooperation between folklorists and those in other scholarly fields is often very profitable. The American Association for State and Local History, for example, has as members those who work with the background facts often needed for the appreciation of folklore. The Linguistic Society of America, the American Anthropological Association, the American Sociological Society, the "Present Day English Group" of the Modern Language Association of America, and the Mississippi Valley Historical Association are a few of the related organizations showing interest in folklore problems and materials. Their publications should be consulted frequently.

Several approaches need emphasis in the current study of American folklore. As the botanist comes to understand plant life through an analysis of the shaping influence of environment, the science of ecology, so folklorists could profit by a careful scrutiny of the situations out of which arise specific songs, tales, proverbial expressions, beliefs, customs, and recreations among various groups of people. The function of folklore, as well as its history, is important. The psychological effects of folklore should be studied by the tracing of responses in specific situations.

The interaction of written and unwritten knowledge is too little understood. How have folk art, music, literature, science, myth influenced the learned tradition and vice versa? Where does one leave off and the other begin?

112

The same type of close stylistic criticism that has been applied to formal literature could profitably be applied to folk tales, folk drama, and folk poetry. How, for example, did the individual narrator imprint his personal outlook and special skill upon a tale or a song, and to what extent did he follow the expected patterns? Sound recordings retain much that the old style pencil and notebook method lost. Then, too, the modern insistence upon adequate documentation for each item collected makes it possible to study the item as a social document as well as an aesthetic contribution.

The growing recognition of the significance of folklore in American life should result in increased attention to the subject in the academic world of scholarship. Anthropologists, historians, sociologists, musicologists, students of literature, art historians and practitioners, race psychologists, and students of international relations all have valuable points of view and useful techniques to contribute. A greater understanding and appreciation of American civilization and of its relationships to mankind in all parts of the world should result from American folklore studies.

Additional References from the *Journal of American Folklore*

I. Recent issues containing biographical sketches of outstanding American folklore scholars:

"Elsie Clews Parsons Memorial Number," 56 (Jan.-March, 1943) ; "Reed Smith, 1881-1943," 56 (October-Dec., 1943) ; "Franz Boas, 1858-1942," 57 (Jan.-March, 1944) ; "Frances Densmore and the Music of the American Indian," 59 (Jan.-March, 1946) ; "John Harrington Cox, 1863-1945" and "Mellinger Edward Henry, 1873-1946," 59 (July-Sept., 1946) ; "Alexander Haggerty Krappe, 1894-1947," 61 (April-June, 1948); "John Avery Lomax, 1867-1948," 61 (July-Sept., 1948) ; "Ruth Fulton Benedict, 1887-1948," 62 (Oct.-Dec., 1949) ; "Salute to Colleague Marius Barbeau," 63 (April-June, 1950).

II. Recent issues containing notices of "Work in Progress," by A. H. Gayton, Herbert Halpert and others:

60 (April-June, 1947) ; 61 (Jan.-March, 1948) ; 62 (Jan.-March, 1949) ; 63 (Jan.-March, 1950).

III. Recent articles surveying folklore studies in different places or subjects:

"Folklore in South America," by Stith Thompson, 61 (July-Sept., 1948) ; "The Current State and Problems of Folklore in Mexico," by Vincente T. Mendoza, 61 (Oct.-Dec., 1948) ; "Folklore and Psychology," by Weston La Barre, 61 (Oct.-Dec., 1948) ; "Folklore Research in North America" by A. H. Gayton and others, 60 (Oct.-Dec., 1947) ; "Conference on the Character and State of Studies in Folklore," sponsored by the American Council of Learned Societies, in Washington, D. C., 1942, 59 (Oct.-Dec., 1946) ; "Folklore after a Hundred Years: a Problem in Redefinition" by Melville J. Herskovits, and "The Problems of Folklore" by Archer Taylor, 59 (April-June, 1946).

IV.   Report on folklore societies:

Wayland D. Hand, "North American Folklore Societies," 56 (July-Sept., 1943) and 59 (Oct.-Dec., 1946) ; and listing of current officers on back covers of every other issue of the *Journal*.

AMERICAN FOLKLORE
SPECIALISTS, 1950
(an incomplete reference list)

I. Myths, Legends, and Traditions

J. Frank Dobie, Austin, Texas
   Texas lore, lost mines, longhorns, etc.
Louise Pound, University of Nebraska
   Midwestern lore, American speech, and the ballad.
Vance Randolph, Eureka Springs, Arkansas
   Ozark lore.
Austin E. Fife, Occidental College
   Mormon lore and songs in the West.
Hector Lee, Chico State College, California
   Nephite and other Mormon lore.
Stanley Edgar Hyman, North Bennington, Vermont
   Myths in American culture.
Ronald L. Ives, Indiana University
   Culture of geographical areas.
Henry Nash Smith, University of Minnesota
   Myths that shaped American life and literature.

II. Folktales and Anecdotes

Stith Thompson, Indiana University
   Folktale motifs, comparative folklore.
Ben A. Botkin, 45 Lexington, Croton-on-Hudson, N. Y.
   Editor and collector.

Harold Thompson, Cornell University
New York state lore.
Mody C. Boatright, University of Texas
Texas humor and tall tales.
Levette J. Davidson, University of Denver
Western tales and lore.
Herbert Halpert, Murray State College, Kentucky
New Jersey, soldier, children, etc.
Ben C. Clough, Brown University
American anecdotes and tales.
Arthur P. Hudson, University of North Carolina
Humor and tales of the South.
William H. Jansen, University of Kentucky
Midwest legends, characters, tales.
Randall Mills, University of Oregon
Tales and frontier lore of the Northwest.
Ernest W. Baughman, University of New Mexico
English and American folk tales.

III. Folk Heroes

Franklin J. Meine, *American People's Encyclopedia,*
Chicago
Mike Fink and other characters, Mississippi River
lore.
Richard M. Dorson, Michigan State College
Davy Crockett, Michigan lore, and colonial lore.
Dr. Moritz Jagendorf, 150 E. 39th, New York City
Johnny Darling, etc.
Paul Beath, Library of Congress, Washington
Febold Feboldson, etc.
Haldeen Braddy, Texas State College, El Paso
Pancho Villa, Texas lore.

Stuart N. Lake, San Diego, California
  Bad men of the West.
Milton Rugoff, Brooklyn, New York
  Folk characters.
Harold W. Fenton
  Pecos Bill, Texas Cowpuncher.

IV. Songs, Ballads, and Rhymes

H. M. Belden, University of Missouri
  Ballads.
Robert W. Gordon, Washington, D. C.
  First curator of Archive of American Folksong.
Alan Lomax, New York City
  Collector and editor, radio programs, recording.
George Pullen Jackson, Vanderbilt University
  Spirituals.
Carl Sandburg, Flatrock, North Carolina
  Collector and singer, *American Songbag*.
Mac Edward Leach, University of Pennsylvania
  Ballads, Sec.-Treas., American Folklore Society.
George Korson, American Red Cross, Washington, D. C.
  Coal camp songs and lore.
Lamar Lunsford, Leicester, North Carolina
  Ballads, folk music, stories.
Emelyn E. Gardner, Claremont, California
  Michigan songs and lore.
E. C. Beck, Central Michigan College
  Lumberjack songs and lore.
Edwin C. Kirkland, University of Florida
  Southern folksongs.
Duncan Emrich, Folklore Archive, Library of Congress
  Director.

Frank Warner, Y.M.C.A., New York City
Songs of Pennsylvania, New York, etc.
Evelyn K. Wells, Wellesley, Massachusetts
Ballads.
Helen Hartness Flanders, Washington, D. C.
Traditional ballads in New England.
Claude M. Simpson, Jr., Ohio State University
Traditional ballads.
W. R. B. Mackenzie, Washington University, St. Louis
Nova Scotia ballads.
John Jacob Niles, Lexington, Kentucky
Singer, collector and arranger.
Alton C. Morris, University of Florida
Songs and ballads of Florida.
Ben Lumpkin, University of Colorado
Songs on records.
Ivan Walton, University of Michigan
Songs and lore of the Great Lakes.
Lester A. Hubbard, University of Utah
Mormon songs.

V. Folk Speech and Folk Sayings

Archer Taylor, University of California
Riddles, proverbs, editor of *Western Folklore*.
Allen Walker Read, Columbia University
American dialect, Britticisms.
Kemp Malone, Johns Hopkins University
American speech.
George P. Wilson, Woman's College, Greensboro, North
Carolina
American dialects.

George W. Stewart, University of California, Berkeley
Place names.
Frederick G. Cassidy, University of Wisconsin
Place names and dialects.
Margaret M. Bryant, Brooklyn College
Proverbs.
M. M. Matthews, University of Chicago Press
Americanisms.
C. E. Voegelin, Indiana University
Linguisitics.
T. M. Pearce, University of New Mexico
Proverbs, place names, legends.
Francis Lee Utley, Ohio State University
Proverbs, folk speech, songs.
D. W. Maurer, University of Louisville
Argots of gamblers, thieves, etc.
Richard Jente, University of North Carolina
Proverbs.
Marjorie M. Kimmerle, University of Colorado
Western linguistic geography.

VI. Customs, Rituals, and Ceremonies

Ruth Benedict, Columbia University
Race and cultural patterns.
C. Grant Loomis, University of California, Berkeley
White magic, word play, etc., editor, *Western Folklore*.
C. L. Sonnichsen, Texas State College, El Paso
Frontier justice, ranch life.
Elaine Lewis, Brooklyn, New York
New York City lore and radio programs.

Clifford Westermeier, Loretto College, Denver
    Rodeo history and lore.
Thomas D. Clark, University of Kentucky
    Frontier life.
Philip D. Jordan, University of Minnesota
    Frontier singers, ways of life, etc.

VII. *Folk Dramas, Festivals, and Holidays*

Sarah Gertrude Knott, 323 So. 12th, Philadelphia
    National Folk Festival, director.
Margot Mayo, New York City
    Folk dances.
Felix Sper, Brooklyn, New York
    Regional drama.
Robert E. Gard, University of Wisconsin
    Folk drama for little theatres.
Lucile K. Czarnowski, University of California, Berkeley
    Dances, Spanish and pioneer.
Frances Gillmor, University of Arizona
    Indian and Mexican drama, southwestern lore.

VIII. *Folk Music, Dances, and Games*

Samuel P. Bayard, Pennsylvania State College
    Fiddle tunes, fife tunes, etc.
Charles Seeger, Pan-American Union, Washington, D. C.
    Musicologist devoted to folk music.
B. H. Bronson, University of California, Berkeley
    Tunes for Child ballads.
Gertrude Kurath, Ann Arbor, Michigan
    Dances.
George Herzog, Indiana University
    Primitive and folk music.

S. B. Hustvedt, University of California, Los Angeles
Ballad music.

Jennie Cossitt, Settlement Assoc., Houston, Texas
Founder, Pipers' Guild of America.

David McIntosh, Southern Illinois University, Carbondale
Old-time games, college songs, and dances.

Sigmund Speath, New York City
Popular music.

IX. *Arts and Crafts*

Elizabeth Burchenal, Folk Arts Center, New York City
Arts and crafts.

Louis C. Jones, New York State Historical Assoc., Cooperstown
Farmer's Museum, New York ghosts, history and
folklore.

F. H. Douglas, Museum of Native Arts, Denver
Indian art.

Mary C. Wheelwright, Santa Fe, New Mexico
Navaho ceremonial art.

Thelma James, Wayne University
City lore, cures, customs.

X. *Spanish-American Folklore*

Aurelio M. Espinosa, Sr. and Jr., Stanford University
Spanish songs, proverbs, drama and tales.

Vincente T. Mendoza, University of Mexico, Mexico City,
D. F.
Mexican songs.

Arthur L. Campa, University of Denver
Songs and stories.

Ralph S. Boggs, University of Miami, Florida
    Latin-American bibliographer and scholar.
Eleanor Hague, Pasadena, California
    Songs.
Frank Goodwyn, University of Maryland
    Songs and tales, Southwest and Chicago area.
Ruben Cobos, University of New Mexico
    Spanish songs.
Juan B. Rael, Stanford University
    Spanish tales in the Southwest.

XI. French-American Folklore

C. M. Barbeau, Victoria Museum, Ottawa
    Canadian French.
Joseph M. Carriére, University of Virginia
    Songs, dialects.
Helen Creighton, Dartmouth, Nova Scotia
    Traditional songs in Nova Scotia.
Calvin A. Claudel, Mississippi State College
    Louisiana songs and stories.
Kewitt Ballowe, Diamond, Louisiana
    Tales and beliefs.

XII. Negro Folklore

Melville J. Herskovits, Northwestern University
    Negro culture.
William R. Bascom, Northwestern University
    Book review editor of *Journal of American Folklore*,
    Cuban lore.

J. Mason Brewer, Samuel Houston College
  Negro anecdotes, etc.
Sterling Brown, Howard University
  Negro songs and poetry.

XIII. *Indian Folklore*

F. W. Hodge, Southwest Museum, Los Angeles
  Indian lore.
Alfred Metraux, Great Neck, New York
  South American Indians.
Clyde Kluckhohn, Peabody Museum, Harvard University
  Indian cultures.
William N. Fenton, Smithsonian Institution, Bureau of
  American Ethnology, Washington, D. C.
  Iroquois music and dance.
Robert H. Lowie, University of California, Berkeley
  Anthropology.
Erminie W. Voegelin, Indiana University
  Folktale.
Ruth Underhill, University of Denver
  Papago, Navaho, and other southwestern tribes.
Margaret Astrov, Correo, New Mexico
  Oral literature.
Ann H. Gayton, University of California, Berkeley
  Indian arts and tales.
A. L. Kroeber, University of California, Berkeley
  Anthropology.
Ralph Linton, Yale University
  Anthropology.
George Foster, Smithsonian Institution, Washington, D.C.
  South American Indian cultures.

XIV. *Other Non-English Folklore*

Alfred L. Shoemaker, Franklin and Marshall College
Pennsylvania Dutch.

Wayland D. Hand, University of California, Los Angeles
Editor, *Journal of American Folklore,* mining lore,
superstitions, German lore.

Ruth Rubin, W. 89th, New York City
Yiddish and Hebrew songs.

Stuart A. Gallacher, Michigan State College
German lore.

Mr. and Mrs. Roman Jakobson, Harvard University
Slavic folklore in New York.

Susie Hoogasian Villa, 709 Cotterel, Detroit
Armenian lore.

Clark M. Garber, Butler, Ohio
Eskimo lore.

Charles Speroni, University of California, Berkeley
Italian lore in America.

Jonas Balys, Indiana University
Lithuanian folklore in U. S.

R. D. Jameson, New Mexico Highlands University
Chinese tales.

XV. *Folklore for Children*

Elizabeth Pilant, Ball State College, Muncie
Folk materials for use of teachers.

Dorothy Howard, Teachers College, Frostburg, Maryland
Folklore in schools.

Ruth Ann Musick, Fairmont State College, West Virginia
Folklore in schools, newspaper columnist, mid-western lore.

Mrs. Ruth Crawford Seeger, c/o Pan-American Union, Washington, D. C.
Folklore for playgrounds and musical settings for folk songs.

Leah Yoffie, Cottey College, Nevada, Missouri
Children's games.

Ray Wood, Raywood, Texas
Rhymes, games, etc.

Richard Chase, Luray, Virginia
Jack tales, songs and dances.

Paul G. Brewster, Henderson State College, Arkadelphia, Arkansas
Games.

Carl Withers, New York City
Songs, games, rhymes, and Cuban lore.

ARCHIVES, MUSEUMS, AND LIBRARIES

The scientific study of folklore, like research in most other fields, is based upon the examination of accumulated collections of data, upon analysis, and upon discussion. In the United States numerous individuals, educational institutions, and other agencies have developed archives, museums, and libraries that specialize in the folklore of words and of music—recorded in print, in manuscript, or on records—and in the folklore of things such as the products of folk arts and crafts as practiced in various regions in different periods.

Probably the most famous archive in the United States is the Folklore Section of the Library of Congress. Established in 1928 as an Archive of American Folk Song, under Robert W. Gordon, it now possesses more than 10,000 different cylinders, discs, and tape recordings of songs and ballads, fiddle tunes, banjo tunes, Indian chants, together with the W.P.A. manuscript collections devoted to folklore. Since the Library of Congress receives for deposit two copies of every copyrighted book published in the United States, its folklore resources in volume form are very great.

Other noteworthy archives of records, manuscripts, or printed matter include the following: the Phillips Barry and Folk Song Society of the Northeast collection, at

Harvard University; the Frank C. Brown manuscript collection, at Duke University, now being edited for publication; the Archive of Vermont folk songs at Middlebury College, sponsored by Helen Hartness Flanders; the Archives of Folk and Primitive Music, developed by Dr. George Herzog, formerly at Columbia University and now at Indiana University; the Archive of the Virginia Folklore Society, under Dr. Arthur Kyle Davis, Jr., at the University of Virginia; and the Negro collections at Fisk University and at Northwestern University. The following individuals have established manuscript or other types of record files that are of special interest: Austin and Alta Fife, Occidental College, Mormon materials; Frances Gillmor and associates at the University of Arizona, southwestern folklore; Thelma James, Wayne University, Detroit, folklore of urban groups; Louis C. Jones, Fenimore House, Cooperstown, New York state lore; Arthur L. Campa and Levette J. Davidson, University of Denver, western and Spanish-American folklore; Herbert N. Halpert, Murray State College, Kentucky and other midwestern lore; Alfred L. Shoemaker, Franklin and Marshall College, Pennsylvania Dutch lore; Alton C. Morris, University of Florida, folksongs; and Harold Thompson, Cornell University, New York state lore.

Folk life museums, such as are to be found in a number of European countries, are still rare in America. If one wishes to see how earlier generations built and furnished their homes, performed the everyday tasks of earning a livelihood, and attempted to add beauty to the utility of their tools, clothing, and utensils, he can visit such restorations or imitations of colonial or pioneer communities as those at Williamsburg, Virginia (although

128

Colonial Williamsburg represents "quality" and wealth rather than folk), at New Salem, Illinois (where Abraham Lincoln tended store), at Dearborn, Michigan (where Henry Ford built "Greenfield Village" to represent a typical pre-automobile era town), and at Sturbridge Village, Massachusetts (a "Living Museum" of early New England). In the Farmers' Museum in Cooperstown, New York, one can see the implements that were used by those who labored for a livelihood with their hands and even watch while a blacksmith demonstrates an almost forgotten folk craft. Many other state or local historical societies have established house museums that exhibit the folk arts of their regions. They should be sought out by the student of folklore.

Among the United States museums with special folk materials are some that emphasize the material tradition of the American Indian; others that have ethnological collections from all over the world; and a few that have preserved the material records of American frontier life or of American occupations. In the first class come the American Museum of Natural History in New York City, the Arizona State Museum in Tucson, the Denver Art Museum, the Museum of the American Indian (Heye Foundation) in New York City, the Museum of Navaho Ceremonial Art in Santa Fe, the Museum of New Mexico in Santa Fe (which is, however, beginning a "Museum of International Folk Art," under Robert Bruce Inverarity), and the Southwest Museum in Los Angeles.

Examples of the second type are the Chicago Natural History Museum (with its Races of Mankind Hall and its numerous collections from all parts of the world), the Peabody Museum of Archeology and Ethnology at Harvard University, and the Thayer Art Museum in Kansas City, Missouri (with its special collection of textiles from all parts of the world, including American quilts, counterpanes and embroideries).

The third class is represented by Fenimore House at Cooperstown (with its permanent exhibit of American Folk Art, assembled by Jean Lipman and others), the Index of American Design in the National Gallery of Art, Washington, D. C., the New Bedford, Massachusetts, Whaling Museum, the Mariners' Museum near Newport News, Virginia, the Museum of Modern Art in New York City (with its collection of nineteenth-century American folk art), and the M. H. de Young Museum in San Francisco (containing materials illustrating the first four decades after the gold rush, together with rooms devoted to early California costumes and to arms and weapons from early times to modern).

Although nearly all public and school libraries contain a number of the best-known books of American folklore, some few universities and city libraries have attempted to develop extensive collections in this field. Among the outstanding are the folklore collections at the University of Indiana, containing over 3,000 volumes in 1946, especially strong in comparative folklore; at the University of North Carolina, about the same number of volumes, but especially strong in Anglo-American and Hispanic-American fields; at the Bucks County Historical Society, Doylestown, Pennsylvania, with much on Pennsylvania-German folklore; at the Cleveland Public Library, containing the John G. White collection of over 80,000 volumes in the field of folklore, Oriental languages, chess and checkers, with much on fables, proverbs, folk songs, romances, gypsies; at the Montclair, New Jersey, Public Library, with its Stella Marek Cushing Fund, which has made possible the purchase of over 1,000 volumes and many pictures, grouped under the headings: "cook books, costume plates, folk dance music, folk songs and books on peasant furniture and folklore"; at the Stefansson Library in New York City, with a hundred books on the folklore of the polar and sub-polar regions; and at the Providence, Rhode Island, Public Library, including the Williams collection of over 1,850 volumes, with emphasis on Irish folklore.

Other strong folklore collections are to be found at the New York Public Library, the New York State College for Teachers in Albany, Harvard University, the University of California in Berkeley and in Los Angeles, the University of Arkansas in Fayetteville, and at many of the libraries of the state historical societies, usually located in the capital of the state. Inquiry locally may lead to the discovery of a fine collection owned by an individual, a local history society, a club, or a private school. In Denver, for example, Frederic H. Douglas, Director of the Museum of Native Arts, has built a fine "working" library of folklore books and magazines, especially rich in the field of Indian Art. In Salt Lake City, the library of the Church of Latter Day Saints has much of value in books, periodicals, and manuscripts concerning pioneer folkways and Mormon customs.

Students will visit the larger collections whenever possible; but even when they cannot go in person, they may be able to obtain needed volumes on short-time loan through the inter-library loan plan. Nearly all of the books listed at the end of each chapter of this guide

131

are still purchasable from the publishers or through book dealers. Every school administrator, community librarian, and research scholar will attempt to extend the collection under his supervision at every opportunity.

References

Chorley, Kenneth, "Colonial Williamsburg." *American Heritage,* Harrisburg, Pa., I, 2 (Winter, 1950), pp. 34-41.

Emrich, Duncan B. M., "Folklore Section of the Library of Congress." *Funk and Wagnalls Standard Dictionary of Folklore, Mythology and Legend,* I, 1949, pp. 407-408.

Handbook of American Museums. The American Association of Museums, Washington, D. C., 1932.

Herzog, George, "Archives of Folk and Primitive Music, Indiana University." *Funk and Wagnalls Standard Dictionary of Folklore, Mythology and Legend.* I, 1949.

Jones, Louis C., "Folklore in the American Heritage." *American Heritage,* Harrisburg, Pa., I, 2 (Winter, 1950), pp. 66-68 and 72.

............, ..., "Folk Culture and the Historical Societies." *American Heritage,* Harrisburg, Pa., I, 3 (Spring, 1950), p. 55.

"Museums—Art—Sciences," in annual volumes of *The World Almanac. New York World-Telegram,* New York City, 1950, etc.

"Old Sturbridge Village: A New England Synthesis in a Unique 'Living Museum.'" *American Heritage,* Harrisburg, Pa., I, 4 (Summer, 1950) pp. 30-39.

Vormelker, Rose L., *Special Library Resources,* 4 Vols. Special Libraries Association, New York, 1941.

34530